Picking the Perfect Cricket Team

To Joanna, William and Oliver

Picking the
Perfect Cricket Team

Benedict Bermange

WHITE OWL

AN IMPRINT OF PEN & SWORD BOOKS LTD.
YORKSHIRE – PHILADELPHIA

First published in Great Britain in 2020 by
White Owl Books
An imprint of
Pen & Sword Books Ltd
Yorkshire – Philadelphia

ISBN 978 1 52676 970 1

Typeset in India by IMPEC eSolutions

Printed and bound in the UK by TJ Books, Padstow, Cornwall

Pen & Sword Books Ltd incorporates the imprints of Pen & Sword Archaeology, Atlas, Aviation, Battleground, Discovery, Family History, History, Maritime, Military, Naval, Politics, Railways, Select, Transport, True Crime, Fiction, Frontline Books, Leo Cooper, Praetorian Press, Seaforth Publishing, Wharncliffe and White Owl.

For a complete list of Pen & Sword titles please contact

PEN & SWORD BOOKS LIMITED
47 Church Street, Barnsley, South Yorkshire S70 2AS, England
E-mail: enquiries@pen-and-sword.co.uk
Website: www.pen-and-sword.co.uk

or

PEN AND SWORD BOOKS
1950 Lawrence Rd, Havertown, PA 19083, USA
E-mail: Uspen-and-sword@casematepublishers.com
Website: www.penandswordbooks.com

Contents

Foreword

We have all done it – argued the relative merits of the all-time great cricketers. With every discussion comes the age-old dilemma of how to compare performances from different generations. The players nowadays are far different – in terms of both technique and stature – to those of yesteryear. There have also been ever-changing conditions of play. Limited-overs cricket has changed the technique of batsmen forever, and the covering of pitches has meant that today's players will never have to face the treachery of a 'sticky dog'.

We all have our lists of greatest players we have played with and against, and we are probably biased towards our own era, which we all view with the rosiest of tinted glasses. Together with these opinions, cricket gives us the facts. We grew up with these numbers, forever etched into the pages of *Wisden*, and we probably all performed slightly better at maths at school thanks to adding up columns in the scorebook and calculating batting and bowling averages at the end of each season.

The long history of cricket is littered with great performances helping to inspire teams to victory. We need look no further than the exploits of Ben Stokes at Leeds in 2019. The Ashes urn may have been retained by Australia over the course of the summer, but for two and a half hours on that Sunday afternoon, it was all about one man's quest for immortality. What helps to make cricket special is how these magical moments happen and who is responsible. The rejoicing in individual feats of brilliance is part of what makes the sport unique.

One of the joys of cricket is that it can be enjoyed as both a team game but also as an individual one. As a captain, I could gain pleasure from the occasions we won a Test even if my own personal contribution had not been that great. Conversely, a different kind of pleasure could be taken – dare I say it – from scoring a century in a losing effort. Cricket enables us to examine its long history without ignoring the individual feats.

Whether or not you believe in the moniker 'Stats are for Prats', statistics have been an integral part of cricket since notchers first carved the score on sticks of hazel. This book consists in the main of arguments and statistical justifications for the best players fulfilling each particular role in the team. I'm an argumentative guy by nature, and how much pleasure you gain from each section will depend in no small measure on how much you enjoy debating cricketers.

You may argue with some of the names presented here, but what cannot be argued with is the way they have been selected. Benedict is the finest statistician I have worked with around the world and the first person I turn to for any kind of statistical query. He also has the great ability to wrap statistics in a meaningful context, and I have no doubt that all the players in this book were considered in great depth before the final selection was made.

Right – now to check my place in the 'Middle-Order Batsmen' section.

Nasser Hussain
October 2020

Introduction

The game of cricket has been played for more than 200 years and much of it has remained unchanged since the earliest days. The stumps are still 22 yards apart, a boundary is still worth 4 runs, and generally – with apologies to Messrs Duckworth & Lewis – if you score more runs at the end of the match, you will win – or draw at the very least!

An incredible volume of cricket statistics is fed to the public daily. At their core, cricket's numbers can inspire, validate true icons of the sport, and at times – much to some people's dismay – transcend the game itself.

One of the great things about cricket's numbers is that the figures themselves become etched in the fabric of the long historical narrative of the game and can be instantly recalled by fans.

Every cricket fan knows what 99.94 means. And 501. For many decades they have known what 10-10 refers to. They don't need any embellishing – the number alone is enough to allow the fan to identify the accomplishment, no matter how long ago the feat was performed.

Some of these numbers have been magical for a long time. Most people would find it difficult to think of more than a few such numbers in any other sport, whereas in cricket it is not hard to think of quite a few with special resonance.

What helps is how well cricket records have been kept. There must have been great speeches made and lost in the mists of time, but we can look back at a game in the 1870s and discover how many wickets Alfred Shaw took, and if he scored any runs or took any catches. We can also discover who was umpiring and what the score was at the fall of each wicket.

However, numbers can only tell you so much. How can we rate a player's standing in one era compared to another based solely on his statistics? Statistics tell the story of how well you did at scoring runs or taking wickets in a match, but can they tell you how well you actually played?

All ranking systems are terrible – except one's own, of course! The mere thought that nearly 150 years of international cricket could be condensed into a top 100 list is just madness – let alone sorting all those players in order. Someone else could reverse the rankings in all the sections and that list could be almost as well justified as the original list.

'You can't compare eras,' is an oft-quoted phrase whenever the relative merits of cricketers are discussed. Be that as it may, it certainly hasn't stopped countless generations of fans sitting around the school playground, dinner table, pub garden or international match debating who the greatest players of all time were.

These discussions tend to revolve around five key factors:

How dominant they were internationally – think Donald Bradman
How dominant they were domestically – think Barry Richards
How good they were at their peak – think Mohammad Yousuf
How long they played – think Wilfred Rhodes
Their overall influence – think Imran Khan

Who didn't enjoy picking their own teams and playing imaginary games with their friends, using either six-sided rollers, cards, dice or tabletop games? And in all of those, a team would be picked to do battle with another.

Fantasy sports started sweeping the world in the 1980s and 1990s, and cricket hopped on board with 'fantasy cricket', a game in which participants could build and manage a virtual team of real county cricketers and would score points using their actual statistics from the season.

Fantasy cricket took some fans' love of the game to new heights by demanding that they took notice of every game taking place all season, since the points acquired by their team could come from any corner of the country – from Durham to Taunton. Of course, if you were a Middlesex fan but owned Dominic Cork in your fantasy team and Middlesex happened to be playing Derbyshire, you wanted him to do well, but you wouldn't want Middlesex to lose. Life could become quite complicated.

Your team would have to be constructed a certain way. You had to begin with two specialist opening batsmen. And that is what they are – specialists. The glamour boys of the middle order would follow – three of them, followed by an all-rounder and a wicketkeeper. The team would be rounded off by four bowlers. And those are the proportions used here – like the proportions in which the players are usually represented in an actual team.

This way, the relative strengths of Jack Hobbs, Sunil Gavaskar and Barry Richards can be debated in isolation, as they would not be competing for playing time with the likes of Don Bradman, Ken Barrington and AB de Villiers. The one slight stumbling block was deciding whether to select two pacemen and two spinners or three paceman and one spinner in the side. To try to solve the conundrum, the Test records of all the bowlers were examined.

To take fifty Test wickets, you need to be a reasonable bowler. There have been 391 bowlers to manage that – of which 246 were seamers, 125 spinners, and the remaining twenty were 'hybrid' bowlers who were able to mix and match their styles – like Garry Sobers, Colin Miller and Tony Greig. Either way, the proportion of seamers to spinners works out pretty much as 2:1, and that is good enough.

To maintain that 2:1 ratio in a group of four bowlers would mean 2.66 seamers and 1.33 spinners. It is impossible to have a fraction of a bowler, but that doesn't need to be an issue, as 100 players are required.

So, each team could be been divided using the following proportions:

2 opening batsmen
3 middle-order batsmen
1 wicketkeeper
1 all-rounder – who would be good enough to make the team as either a batsman or bowler
2.66 seamers
1.33 spinners

Making a total of eleven players.

Out of a total population of 100 players, those proportions work out as follows – exactly and rounded to the nearest whole number:

18.2 opening batsmen	(18)
27.3 middle-order batsmen	(27)
9.1 wicketkeepers	(9)
9.1 all-rounders	(9)
24.2 seamers	(24)
12.1 spinners	(12)

Making a total of 100 players exactly – or 99 players if the rounded numbers are used, which is somewhat frustrating. However, as all the actual calculated numbers are slightly higher than their rounded values, each reader is mathematically justified to add a favourite player who didn't make the original cut. Call it the 'reader's privilege'.

All statistics are correct as of 25 August 2020.

Chapter 1
Opening Batsmen

Jack Hobbs   **international career 1908–30**

'The sound of his bat somehow puts me in mind of vintage port.' A.A. Milne

On 16 December 1922, Jack Hobbs turned 40 years old. He was already acknowledged as the greatest batsman in the game, inheriting that mantle from W.G. Grace, and had ninety-nine first-class centuries to his name. For many players, that might have been the start of their twilight years, but not so for Hobbs.

Never has the mantra 'Life begins at 40' been more apt. From then until the end of his career, he stroked another hundred centuries and improved his batting average from 45.93 at the time of his birthday to its final figure of 50.70.

The eldest of twelve children, his father was appointed groundsman and resident umpire at Jesus College, Cambridge. The young Hobbs' first introduction to cricket was watching the touring Australians play Cambridge University at Fenner's at the tender age of eighteen months.

He arrived in first-class cricket in 1905 at the height of cricket's 'Golden Age' – an era of Ranji, of Trumper and of Fry. He had no formal coaching but brought with him expert front-foot play and a high backlift, enabling his back-foot strokes to be equally effective. His elegance could have fitted into any cricketing age and he had equal mastery over both pace and spin bowling.

When Hobbs played his first major match for Surrey, the opponents were Gentlemen of England, captained by W.G. Grace. Impressed by the youngster's score of 88 in the Surrey second innings, Grace's view was clear: 'He's goin' to be a good 'un.' In 1925, Hobbs passed Grace's tally of first-class centuries and then subsequently passed his runs record too, ending up with more first-class runs and centuries than anyone else in history.

Player	Runs	100s
J.B. Hobbs	**61,760**	**199**
F.E. Woolley	**58,959**	145
E.H. Hendren	**57,611**	170
C.P. Mead	**55,061**	153
W.G. Grace	**54,211**	124
H. Sutcliffe	**50,670**	151
W.R. Hammond	**50,551**	167

If one of the measures of a successful opener is his ability to see off the new ball, Hobbs ranks higher than any other batsman in Test history who batted at least fifty times in terms of his ability to reach double figures.

Player	Innings	10+	%
J.B. Hobbs	**102**	**88**	**86.27**
H. Sutcliffe	84	71	**84.52**
J.B. Stollmeyer	56	47	**83.92**
D.G. Bradman	80	66	**82.50**
E.J. Barlow	57	47	**82.45**

Hobbs also had to cope with what was probably the first example of extreme media scrutiny as he chased down and then overtook W.G. Grace's then accepted record of 126 first-class centuries. Ten thousand spectators packed the County Ground at Taunton in 1925 as he equalled the record with a score of 101 in the first innings and celebrated with a ginger ale. For good measure, he then scored another century in the second innings to make the record his own.

He missed four full seasons due to the war, missing active service to work in a munitions factory and coach at Westminster School. Ironically, his final tally of runs could have been even greater as he was in prime form when war broke out. From the start of the 1913 English domestic season in May up to the end of the following summer, when stumps were drawn at the start of September, he played seventy-seven first-class matches, scoring 6,791 runs at an average of 57.55, with twenty-five centuries.

Post-war he became more of an accumulator than an artist, and his tally of first-class runs and centuries will remain records until the end of time. He was an outstanding fielder and runner between the wickets, and his ability to score runs on the most unpredictable of wickets caused many to rate him even higher than Don Bradman.

Cricket has given us such nicknames as 'Master Blaster' and 'Little Master' but to this day, only one player has been referred to as 'The Master' – and that was Hobbs. Hobbs is remembered as much for his modesty and kindness as he is for his run-scoring. Perhaps no other player was so universally admired, and in 1953 he became the first professional cricketer to be knighted for services to the game.

Len Hutton   **international career 1937–55**

'Hutton was never dull. His bat was part of his nervous system. His play was sculptured. His forward defensive stroke was a complete statement.' Harold Pinter

Len Hutton's Test career started with scores of 0 and 1 against New Zealand at Lord's in 1937. He put things right in the very next Test with an innings of 100 at Lord's and from that moment on, he never looked back. Just a year later, he played the highest and arguably the most famous innings ever by an England batsman when he broke the world record for the highest Test score with 364 against Australia at The Oval.

Score	Player	Against	Venue	Year
364	**L. Hutton**	**Australia**	**The Oval**	**1938**
336*	W.R. Hammond	New Zealand	Auckland	1933
333	G.A. Gooch	India	Lord's	1990
325	A. Sandham	West Indies	Kingston	1930
310*	J.H. Edrich	New Zealand	Leeds	1965

It wasn't just the highest individual score for England, it was an innings lasting 13 hours 17 minutes, and thanks to the faster over rates of the 1930s, he batted through 292 overs, facing a total of 847 deliveries. Not out on 300 at the end of the second day of this timeless match, he would have endured a sleepless night with Don Bradman's Ashes record of 334 and Wally Hammond's Test record of 336 not out within his grasp. It was just his sixth Test and the world appeared to be at his feet, but just a year later, war broke out and Hutton volunteered for service.

In March 1941, he found himself in a York gym preparing for the forthcoming raid of Dieppe. A mat slipped from under him and he fractured his left arm and dislocated his wrist. His future cricket career lay in the hands of the surgeons and, post-operation, his left arm was 2 inches shorter than his right. Fortunately, the accident didn't have a lasting effect on his batting abilities.

	Matches	Runs	Avge	100s
Pre-war	177	11,658	48.98	36
Post-war	336	28,482	58.72	93

England were trounced in the 1946/47 Ashes series, but Hutton made an undefeated 122 in the final Test at Sydney, which gave some indication of the riches to come. Runs flowed the following summer but the Ashes were again lost against the all-conquering 1948 invincible Australians.

Throughout this time, despite the emergence of his teammates Denis Compton and Bill Edrich, England's batting relied on Hutton possibly more than anyone before or since. More than a hundred batsmen have scored more than a thousand runs for England. Of all of them, Hutton scored the highest percentage of his team's runs when in the team. He was the only one who successfully mastered both 'twin threats' at the time of Lindwall and Miller (often with a second new ball after just fifty-five overs), and Ramadhin and Valentine.

Player	Matches	Runs	%
L. Hutton	**79**	**6,971**	**18.20**
J.B. Hobbs	61	5,410	**17.91**
H. Sutcliffe	54	4,555	**17.24**
W.R. Hammond	85	7,249	**16.91**
K.F. Barrington	82	6,806	**16.74**

Double-hundreds followed in both the summers of 1949 and 1950, and in 1952 he was appointed the first professional England captain. The move paid off as England finally regained the Ashes the following year after nineteen years of hurt, before retaining them eighteen months later down under, which was the crowning glory of his cricketing career. He had six series in charge, winning five and drawing the other.

Unlike Hobbs, for whom life literally began at 40, Hutton hung up his boots at the end of the 1955 season at the age of 39, troubled by back pain. He moved into journalism and worked for an engineering firm until his 'second' retirement at the age of 68.

Graham Gooch   international career 1975–95

'He is built like a guardsman and that expressionless face with the black moustache surely saw service in England's imperial wars, defending Rorke's Drift and marching up the Khyber Pass.' Geoffrey Moorhouse

For a man whose Test career started with a 'pair' to graduate to become the leading run-scorer in top-level cricket (First-class + List A + Twenty20) in history is remarkable, but few men have enjoyed batting as much as Graham Gooch.

Player	Runs
G.A. Gooch	**67,057**
G.A. Hick	**64,372**
J.B. Hobbs	**61,760**
F.E. Woolley	**58,959**
G. Boycott	**58,521**

His career transcended generations as he faced off with the finest of the 1970s, 1980s and the 1990s, and often came out on top. No batsman who endured a pair on debut ended up with more Test runs.

Player	Team	Runs
G.A. Gooch	**Eng**	**8,900**
M.S. Atapattu	SL	**5,502**
Saeed Anwar	Pak	**4,052**
D. Elgar	SA	**3,888**
K.R. Rutherford	NZ	**2,465**
G.S. Ramchand	Ind	**1,180**

He was a pioneer too: he was one of the first players to have a high back-lift, which is now so common the world over, and he was obsessed with fitness, which put him at odds with some of his teammates at the time. After his initial two Test appearances, he worked hard to get back into the team. This took him three years, but once established he was an automatic selection when available – although he missed three years of international cricket due to leading a rebel tour of South Africa. He returned in glory, helping England regain the Ashes in 1985, and he eventually became captain after the disastrous 1989 Ashes series under David Gower, in which Gooch had asked to be dropped after Terry Alderman seemed to be able to dismiss him at will.

He had always been a colossus at county level, scoring prolifically in all the domestic tournaments for his beloved Essex, but at the time his Test average stood as a decidedly underachieving 36.90 from seventy-three Tests over fourteen years. At the age of 36, he may have been a short-term captaincy choice.

However, he was at his best with the bat with the additional responsibility thrust upon him, averaging 58.72, including his memorable double of 333 and 123 against India at Lord's in 1990. That golden summer brought him 1,058 runs in six Tests – despite having been dismissed by Richard Hadlee to the first ball he faced.

Without doubt his finest effort was an unbeaten 154 against the West Indies at Leeds the following year, carrying his bat through England's second innings of 252, in which no one else scored more than 27. He saw off Ambrose, Patterson, Walsh and Marshall, leading England to a memorable victory.

He was unfortunate to captain an England team who were unable to live up to his own high standards, and he found that a cause of great frustration. He eventually resigned at the age of 40 in the middle of another Ashes defeat but was still a good enough player to score 673 runs in the series – more than anyone else from either side. Three years later, he led all-comers with nearly 2,000 runs in the County Championship.

Despite losing three years to his South African ban, his subsequent late career blooming saw him retire as England's leading Test run-scorer, a tally currently only surpassed – to his delight – by his own protégé, Alastair Cook, who shared the same single-minded love of batting that Gooch did.

After eventual retirement, he coached Essex and also served as England's batting coach. Former adversary Shane Warne summed him up perfectly: 'Graham Gooch was the English equivalent of our Allan Border, and that is almost the highest praise I can give to a cricketer.'

Sunil Gavaskar   **international career 1971–87**

'Perhaps it is best to say that, if all living things in India are incarnations, Gavaskar is technical orthodoxy made flesh.' Scyld Berry

It is said that Sachin Tendulkar may have had the weight of a billion people's expectations sitting squarely on his shoulders, but the only thing that he had over Sunil Gavaskar is that the population of India in 1971 – when Gavaskar started his Test career – was a 'mere' 566 million.

No one has had a more extraordinary first series in Test cricket, and that start came in 1971 against the West Indies, setting the tone for his career to come. His first runs in Test cricket came by way of two non-signalled leg byes from the bowling of Vanburn Holder, but he was away.

By the time the four matches had been completed he had accumulated 774 runs at an average of 154.80, culminating in 124 and 220 in the final Test at Trinidad. Suddenly, India had a player who could play fast bowling! Their earlier heroes were masters of the turning ball but struggled once confronted with much more than medium pace. And what a time it was for fast bowlers – Lillee, Thomson, Hogg, Willis, Botham, Hadlee and Imran were all at their peak, not to mention any number of terrifying pacemen from the Caribbean.

Perhaps people should not have been surprised as Gavaskar was named the Indian Schoolboy Cricketer of the Year in 1966, a year in which he scored two double centuries for his team.

The first man to reach 10,000 Test runs and the man who overtook Don Bradman's record of twenty-nine Test hundreds was a diminutive man. He had an impeccable defence but was also more than capable of playing his strokes, and his record against the all-conquering West Indian sides of the 1970s and 1980s marked him as one of the greats. No one in the history of Test cricket has scored more runs against the West Indies than he did.

Player	Team	Matches	Runs	Avge	100s
S.M. Gavaskar	**Ind**	**27**	**2,749**	**65.45**	**13**
J.H. Kallis	SA	24	**2,356**	73.62	8
G. Boycott	Eng	29	**2,205**	45.93	5
G.A. Gooch	Eng	26	**2,197**	44.83	5
S.R. Waugh	Aus	32	**2,192**	49.81	7

Ironically, for someone who made his name as an opening batsman, in his earlier career he was also called upon to open the bowling on seven occasions. In an era when India's focus was on spin, he bowled in a total of twenty-nine Test innings, taking a grand total of one wicket. But what a wicket it was – Zaheer Abbas at Faisalabad in 1978, when he was just 4 runs short of his second century in the match.

Gavaskar had the nation's hopes on his shoulders for most of his career. His was the wicket the opposition valued the most and if he were to bat all day and remain not out at the close, India still had hope, no matter how many runs he had scored. His 221 at The Oval in 1979 nearly brought a famous triumph and the whole nation celebrated as he took a quick single against Pakistan on 7 March 1987 to become the first batsman to score 10,000 Test runs.

Player	Year
S.M. Gavaskar	**1987**
A.R. Border	**1993**
S.R. Waugh	**2003**
B.C. Lara	**2004**
S.R. Tendulkar	**2005**

His final Test innings of 96 on a minefield at Bengaluru was as much of a masterpiece as anyone who witnessed it had ever seen. However, few performances would have given him as much pleasure as his solitary ODI century – coming as it did in a World Cup match against New Zealand at Nagpur in what would be his penultimate match.

His stumps may have been rearranged by Malcolm Marshall at the end of the fourth day of the MCC Bicentenary Match, but his first-innings 188 ensured that those who saw it would never forget his contribution to his final first-class match.

Herbert Sutcliffe   international career 1924–35

'Herbert Sutcliffe needed some getting out. He was a great battler for England and for Yorkshire. He never gave his wicket away – unless he was satisfied he had made enough already.' Harold Larwood

In recent years, various England batsmen have taken great pains to point out that their under-fire colleagues still average 40 in Test cricket. Herbert Sutcliffe averaged 60. And not only that, he always averaged 60 – or more – throughout his fifty-four-match Test career. It could have been even better, as his last fourteen Tests brought an average of just 35.80 after his first forty had seen sixteen centuries. Only six batsmen in Test history have always averaged at least 45, and Sutcliffe is top of the pile.

Player	Team	Matches	Lowest
H. Sutcliffe	**Eng**	**54**	**60.73**
Javed Miandad	Pak	124	**51.75**
F.M.M. Worrell	WI	51	**49.49**
S.M. Gavaskar	Ind	125	**47.70**
K.D. Walters	Aus	74	**47.03**
H.L. Collins	Aus	19	**45.07**

He had an inauspicious start. Orphaned by the age of 10, he was brought up by his austere aunt above a bakery in Pudsey. It would have been impossible for such an upbringing not to influence the young boy, and his batting – prolific though it was – never had the carefree attitude of his long-time opening partner Jack Hobbs.

His first-class career was exactly bookended by the two world wars and he wasted no time fitting into the Yorkshire side in the unique two-day County Championship season of 1919. From then on, he was a permanent feature of the side and he was Denis Compton's predecessor as the possessor of the sleekest hair in cricket.

He was not a stylist with the bat and was frequently overshadowed by his illustrious teammates Hobbs and Wally Hammond, but there was no denying the effectiveness of his method. He could guts it out with the best of them if conditions dictated, and they frequently did against the likes of Grimmett and O'Reilly – two of the best spinners in cricket history. He did not have the classic Hammond cover drive, but really came into his own on difficult wickets.

His twin efforts of 76 and 161 won the 1926 Oval Test, which ensured a 1-0 Ashes series victory for England, as the first four Tests in the series had all ended drawn. Until the epic Ben Stokes-inspired effort at Leeds in the summer of 2019, England's highest successful fourth-innings run-chase in their Test history was the 332-7 they managed at Melbourne in the early days of 1929. On that occasion, Sutcliffe scored 135 in six and a half hours, and only departed when England needed just 14 more to win and seal the Ashes.

Despite his record first wicket partnership of 555 with Percy Holmes against Essex in 1932, it is with Jack Hobbs that he is most fondly remembered. In terms of average runs per partnership it is still the most fruitful in Test history, with a minimum of twenty-five partnerships.

Partners	Partnerships	Runs	Avge	100s
J.B. Hobbs & H. Sutcliffe (Eng)	39	3,249	87.81	15
J.L. Langer & R.T. Ponting (Aus)	48	3,451	82.16	14
Mohammad Yousuf & Younis Khan (Pak)	42	3,137	78.42	9
AB de Villiers & J.H. Kallis (SA)	44	3,108	75.80	13
Javed Miandad & Mudassar Nazar (Pak)	28	2,117	75.60	10

Geoffrey Boycott   international career 1964–82

'He built a fortress around himself, in life as at the wicket.' Christopher Martin-Jenkins

He may be a bit of a cliché nowadays, and by all accounts his mother was an even greater player – even with a stick of rhubarb – but there is no denying the fact that for more than two decades, Geoffrey Boycott was a leading figure in English cricket.

It was not always for good reasons: throughout his career there were plenty of run-ins and run-outs. He managed to frequently fall foul of the Yorkshire committee and his selfish batting won him no favours from the England selectors, who dropped him from the team after an undefeated 246 against India at Leeds in 1967. He was never seen as a team player, never more exemplified than when Basil D'Oliveira confided to him that he had finally figured out how to read the mystery Australian spinner Johnny Gleeson. Boycott replied: 'I've known for a week, but don't tell the others.'

Despite all of this, he still ended his career with more runs and centuries in first-class cricket than anyone else to have debuted since the Second World War.

Player	Runs	100s
G. Boycott	**48,426**	**151**
T.W. Graveney	**47,793**	**122**
G.A. Gooch	**44,846**	**128**
D.L. Amiss	**43,423**	**102**
M.C. Cowdrey	**42,719**	**107**

Even now, more than thirty years after he finally hung up his bat, he still polarises opinion, and remains a much-in-demand commentator around the world.

He would probably have beaten Sunil Gavaskar to the 10,000 Test run mark had he not self-imposed an exile of thirty Tests over the course of his career, or gone to South Africa with the England rebel tourists in 1981/82 when still scoring heavily enough in county cricket to retain his spot at the top of the England order.

Ian Botham had certainly had enough of Boycott's self-obsession with crease occupation on the 1977/78 tour of New Zealand, when he was sent in up the order to put an end to Boycott's stonewalling when England were on the hunt for quick runs. Under instructions from vice-captain Bob Willis, he succeeded in calling Boycott for a quick single and running him out.

It made no difference. He virtually batted himself to a standstill in the 1978/79 Ashes series, in which he faced 569 deliveries between boundaries, encompassing six innings, which included his entire 337-ball effort of 77 at Perth.

The defining moment of his career was played out in front of his home Leeds fans in the 1977 Ashes series when an on drive brought up his 100th first-class century. But despite all his records (he retired as the leading Test run-scorer of all time), the one he points out first is that he held the record for the highest individual score in a Lord's one-day final – an innings of 146 against Surrey in 1965 – for more than fifty years.

Score	Player	Match	Year
187*	A.D. Hales	Nottinghamshire v Surrey	2017
146	**G. Boycott**	**Yorkshire v Surrey**	**1965**
144*	M.D. Stoneman	Surrey v Nottinghamshire	2017
132*	I.V.A. Richards	Somerset v Surrey	1981
128*	M.T.G. Elliott	Yorkshire v Somerset	2002

Love him or loathe him, it was impossible to ignore him for the past half-century. And he has no intention of slipping away quietly anytime soon!

Virender Sehwag   **international career 1999–2013**

'The greatest destroyer since the U-boat.' Ian Chappell

It may seem strange now, but there was a time in the mid-1990s and early 2000s when India struggled to find a settled opening partnership in Test cricket. The likes of Sadagoppan Ramesh, Shiv Sunder Das, Wasim Jaffer and Vikram Rathore were tried and discarded before a diminutive batsman from Najafgarh was given the nod.

In the 1,563 Tests until Virender Sehwag hit 105 on his Test debut at Bloemfontein in 2001, openers in Test cricket had scored their runs at an overall strike rate of 41.43. Among them were famed stonewallers like Boycott, Atherton and Lawry, but also included were more flamboyant players like Greenidge, Srikkanth and Trumper. Sehwag scored his runs at twice that overall rate – 82.23 runs per hundred balls. He revolutionised the opener's position in Test cricket and ended up scoring more runs at a greater rate than anyone with at least 2,000 Test runs in history.

Player	Team	Runs	Strike Rate
V. Sehwag	**Ind**	**8,586**	**82.23**
A.C. Gilchrist	Aus	5,570	**81.96**
Kapil Dev	Ind	5,248	**80.99**
D.A. Warner	Aus	7,244	**72.85**
Sarfaraz Ahmed	Pak	2,657	**70.98**

He flew firmly in the face of tradition – his foot movement was minimal against the seamers, but his eye extraordinarily good and his mantra of 'see ball, hit ball' served him well over the course of his career. Despite the unorthodox methods, his head was totally still, and when he did move his feet, they only moved after the ball had been delivered.

India had never had a Test triple-hundred but in March 2004, Sehwag found himself on 295 not out facing Saqlain Mushtaq at Multan. At the back of his mind might have been his failure to clear the boundary when on 195 at the Melbourne Cricket Ground against Australia three months earlier. Pressure? What pressure? With one huge swing of the bat the landmark was his. Four years later, for good measure he scored another triple – this time against the South African attack of Steyn, Ntini, Morkel and Kallis. On that occasion, he reached his 300 from just 278 deliveries.

Incredibly, he almost made it three Test triple-centuries the following year, but he fell 7 runs short against Sri Lanka at Mumbai. He had to console himself with the most runs in a day of Test cricket since the Second World War, and the third-most in history.

Player	Runs	Match	Venue	Year
D.G. Bradman	**309**	Australia v England	Leeds	1930
W.R. Hammond	**295**	England v New Zealand	Auckland	1933
V. Sehwag	**284**	**India v Sri Lanka**	**Mumbai (BS)**	**2009**
D.C.S. Compton	**273**	England v Pakistan	Nottingham	1954
D.G. Bradman	**271**	Australia v England	Leeds	1934

Perhaps surprisingly, his teammate Sachin Tendulkar beat him to becoming the first batsman to score a double-century in ODI cricket, but Sehwag followed him to the mark the following year, setting a record score of 219, which stood for three years. He helped India win the World Cup in 2011, hitting the first ball of the match for four on five different occasions over the course of the tournament.

Barry Richards   **international career 1970**

'I have never seen better driving since Hammond.' E.D.R. Eagar

With Barry Richards it will always be a case of 'what might have been'. Never mind the 28,258 first-class runs at an average of 54.74, or the eighty first-class centuries, how might he have fared had he been able to continue his Test career beyond the mere four Tests he was allowed by circumstances beyond his control? Despite the mountains of runs he made, his name is always mentioned with others who, for one reason or other, were unable to continue their international careers, some of whom are listed below. It is always fascinating to try to project how their careers would have panned out had fate not stepped in their way.

Nari Contractor
Ben Hollioake
Phil Hughes
Archie Jackson
Vinod Kambli
Craig Kieswetter
Barry Richards
Collie Smith
James Taylor
Ken Wadsworth

What we do know is that he scored 508 runs in those four Tests. Only eight batsmen in the history of the game have scored that many or more in their first four Tests.

Player	Team	Runs
S.M. Gavaskar	Ind	774
G.A. Headley	WI	703
C.C. Hunte	WI	577
Javed Miandad	Pak	573
V.G. Kambli	Ind	544
K.S. Ranjitsinhji	Eng	516
H.L. Collins	Aus	515
B.A. Richards	**SA**	**508**

Four of them – Gavaskar, Headley, Javed and Ranji – can be considered all-time greats. Conrad Hunte ended his career with a Test average of 45.06 from forty-four Tests and was subsequently knighted. Herbie Collins averaged 63 in his first twelve Tests but just 17.50 in his last seven. Vinod Kambli's career followed a similar path as two double-centuries in his first four Tests and an average of 113.28 after seven Tests suggested a path to greatness. However, his last ten Tests brought an average of just 22.38 and he was discarded for good less than three years after his debut.

With a Test career over almost before it had started, he had to make do with prolific feats of scoring in domestic cricket around the world. He lit up World Series Cricket with an innings of 207 at Perth in 1978, and scored a century before lunch on nine occasions – a modern-day record, and only bettered by batsmen who plied their trade in the early years of the twentieth century.

Player	100s
J.B. Hobbs	16
G.L. Jessop	14
F.E. Woolley	13
K.S. Ranjitsinhji	10
W.G. Grace	9
B.A. Richards	9

For Hampshire, he entertained fans for a decade, averaging more than 50 and forming a formidable opening partnership with Gordon Greenidge. He wasted no time acclimatising to English conditions, as he passed 2,000 runs in his first season, topping all run-scorers in the County Championship in 1968.

He had a season with South Australia in 1970/71 and it was for them that he played arguably his most famous innings. On the bouncy WACA track at Perth, facing an opposition bowling line-up featuring Graham McKenzie, Dennis Lillee and Tony Lock, he hit 356 in six and a quarter hours, 325 of them on the first day alone. In that season's Sheffield Shield, he scored 1,145 runs in eight matches – nearly 400 runs more than anyone else.

Which way was Richards headed? We will never know. That question is one of the great unknowns in cricket history. The consolation for cricket fans around the world was that he stuck around long enough to give entertainment to the watching crowds wherever he played.

Alastair Cook   international career 2006–18

'What he has brought to the dressing room, the team, what he has done for English cricket as a player and captain is above and beyond.' James Anderson

The world first woke up to Alastair Cook in the summer of 2000. The Costcutter Under-15s World Challenge took place in England and he was selected for the England team, along with other future stars Tim Bresnan, James Hildreth and Samit Patel. Still a pupil at Bedford School at the time, he failed to set the world alight, but remained on England's radar, and by the time the Under-19 World Cup rolled around four years later in Bangladesh, he was captain.

Two centuries flowed from his bat in the tournament and it was only a matter of time before the senior side came knocking. Marcus Trescothick had departed from England's 2006 tour of India prematurely and the call went out to Cook – who was in the Caribbean with England's 'A' team – to fly in on a three-day journey and land straight into the team.

A debut century sealed his place in the side, and perhaps even more remarkable than his feats of run-scoring was his durability. After missing what would have been his third Test with a stomach bug, he never missed another, setting a record of 159 successive Tests.

He was part of a highly successful opening partnership with Andrew Strauss, which continued the strong tradition going back more than a century of an England senior partner able to pass on the knowledge to a more junior partner, which ended with Cook.

Grace and Rhodes
Rhodes and Hobbs
Hobbs and Sutcliffe
Sutcliffe and Hutton
Hutton and Cowdrey
Cowdrey and Boycott
Boycott and Gooch
Gooch and Atherton
Atherton and Trescothick
Trescothick and Strauss
Strauss and Cook
Cook and a whole heap of others

Cook's career was a triumph of putting substance over style. His runs were a product of the age-old adage of 'batting time'. The longer he batted, the more runs he scored – never more so than in the 2010/11 Ashes series, in which he batted for nearly thirty-six hours and scored 766 runs. He also mastered Asian conditions, scoring more runs on that continent than any other visiting batsman.

Player	Team	Matches	Runs	Avge	100s
A.N. Cook	**Eng**	**28**	**2,710**	**53.13**	**9**
J.H. Kallis	SA	25	**2,058**	55.62	8
R.T. Ponting	Aus	28	**1,889**	41.97	5
H.M. Amla	SA	25	**1,859**	47.66	7
S. Chanderpaul	WI	27	**1,850**	48.68	4

Even though he brought the curtain down on his Test career at the age of 'just' 33, due to his early start, he owned most of the major England batting records. Most caps? Check. Most runs? Check. Most centuries? Check. Most matches as captain? Check. Most catches in the field? Check. Perhaps inevitably, he ended his Test career the way it started – with a half-century and a century, to end as the leading left-handed Test run-scorer of all time.

Name	Team	Matches	Runs	Avge
A.N. Cook	**Eng**	**161**	**12,468**	**45.33**
K.C. Sangakkara	SL	134	**12,400**	57.40
B.C. Lara	WI	131	**11,953**	52.88
S. Chanderpaul	WI	164	**11,867**	51.37
A.R. Border	Aus	156	**11,174**	50.56

Chris Gayle   international career 1999–2019

'You can't exactly put a fielder in the car park, can you?' Ravi Bopara

Like him or not, Chris Gayle certainly had talent and could entertain a crowd like no other modern batsman. He made the modern Twenty20 format his own with 2,500 more runs than anyone else in the format and far more centuries. History will probably remember him for his feats in shorter forms of the game, but it is easy to forget that before Twenty20 Chris Gayle there was Test match Chris Gayle.

Before his first Twenty20 match on 15 September 2005, he had played fifty-two Tests with a batting average of just under 40. Only four months earlier, he had amassed a ten-and-a-half-hour 317 against South Africa on an admittedly featherbed Antigua Recreation Ground pitch, but the application was there for all to see. In November 2010, he batted even longer and even higher as Sri Lanka were tamed to the tune of 333 at Galle, of which a record 143 came off Suraj Randiv.

Runs	Batsman	Bowler	Match	Venue	Year
143	**C.H. Gayle**	**S. Randiv**	**SL v WI**	**Galle**	**2010**
136	L. Hutton	L. O'B Fleetwood-Smith	Eng v Aus	The Oval	1938
130	B.C. Lara	G.J. Batty	WI v Eng	St John's	2004
125	D.P.M.D. Jayawardene	N. Boje	SL v SA	Colombo (SSC)	2006
118	G.S. Sobers	Fazal Mahmood	WI v Pak	Kingston	1958
118	G.S. Sobers	Khan Mohammad	WI v Pak	Kingston	1958

There were smatterings of other highlights too in the longest form of the game. A good enough spinner to boast two five-wicket hauls in Test cricket, there was a taste of things to come when he hit Matthew Hoggard for six fours in an over in the 2004 Oval Test. He also – perhaps unsurprisingly – became the first batsman to strike the first ball of a Test for six at Dhaka in 2012.

But then came fortune and fame, and thanks to disinterest and various disputes with the West Indies Cricket Board, his Test appearances dwindled and his last appearance in that form was in 2014.

He didn't mind: the self-anointed 'Universe Boss' set about destroying attacks in the shortest form of the game around the world. Records continued to fall to his broad bat – a thirty-ball Twenty20 century for Royal Challengers Bangalore, and in 2015, he scored the first World Cup double-century, making him the first player to achieve the triumvirate of Test 300, ODI 200 and T20I 100. He also became the first player to hit 500 sixes in all forms of senior cricket.

Player	Sixes
C.H. Gayle	**534**
Shahid Afridi	**476**
R.G. Sharma	**423**
B.B. McCullum	**398**
MS Dhoni	**359**

He has scored more than 13,000 runs in Twenty20 cricket, plying his trade in eleven different countries around the world. That tally is a proverbial mile ahead of anyone else. And his twenty-two centuries are also a long way clear of the chasing pack.

Even when he became pretty much immobile in the field, he was still an automatic pick for both club and country, as his taming of the England attack in early 2019 with 424 runs and thirty-nine sixes in five matches bore witness to, possibly making up for his deficiencies in running between the wickets.

Graeme Smith   international career 2002–14

'Graeme Smith was such a good batsman, we had five team meetings just to try to contain him – and failed miserably.' Michael Vaughan

When Graeme Smith had the captaincy of South Africa thrust upon his broad shoulders after the home side's disappointing showing in their home World Cup in 2003, he had just eight Test matches under his belt and became the third-youngest (and still just the fifth-youngest) Test captain in history.

His first major assignment was the 2003 tour of England and he could not have dreamed of how things would pan out. He struck 277 in the opening Test at Edgbaston – then a national record – and followed up with 259 in the next Test at Lord's. That innings remains the highest score by any opposition batsman at the ground, surpassing a record held for nearly three quarters of a century by Don Bradman.

Score	Player	Team	Year
259	**G.C. Smith**	**South Africa**	**2003**
254	D.G. Bradman	Australia	1930
215	S.P.D. Smith	Australia	2015
214*	C.G. Greenidge	West Indies	1984
206*	W.A. Brown	Australia	1938
206	M.P. Donnelly	New Zealand	1949

He was not grace personified, eschewing a left-hander's natural artistry for pure muscle power; his closed bat turned to the leg side was never described as elegant, however effective it might have been. He shared a dressing room in this new 'golden era' of South African cricket with others who received more of the batting plaudits, such as Hashim Amla, Jacques Kallis and AB de Villiers. However, it was Smith's immense physical presence that perhaps gave the most reassurance to South African fans around the world.

South Africa had not beaten England in a Test series in England since 1965, but Smith was determined to put that right in 2008. With his side one match up in the series after victory at Headingley, they found themselves chasing 281 to win on a tricky Edgbaston pitch. They were soon in trouble at 93-4 but Smith stood firm, leading the victory charge with an unbeaten 154, which included 99 runs in the final session of the fourth day. That winter, the South Africans conquered Australia, with another Smith century inspiring a successful fourth-innings chase of 414 at Perth.

He led South Africa to another series win in England in 2012, this time toppling their hosts from the number one spot in the Test rankings and scoring a century in the victory at The Oval, a win in which South Africa only lost two wickets. In doing so, he saw off a third successive England captain as Nasser Hussain, Michael Vaughan and Andrew Strauss all ended their time in charge after failing to defeat the Proteas under Smith.

He kept on for another couple of years, becoming the first player to captain his side in a hundred Tests and the first to win fifty of them.

Captain	Team	Matches	Won	Lost	Tied	Drawn
G.C. Smith	**SA**	**109**	**53**	**29**	**0**	**27**
A.R. Border	Aus	93	32	22	1	38
S.P. Fleming	NZ	80	28	27	0	25
R.T. Ponting	Aus	77	48	16	0	13
C.H. Lloyd	WI	74	36	12	0	26
MS Dhoni	Ind	60	27	18	0	15

Victor Trumper   **international career 1899–1912**

'He was as modest as he was magnificent: batting seemed to be just part of himself.' Pelham Warner

The subject of surely the most famous photograph of a batsman in history, Victor Trumper's lasting fame was not generated by mere figures alone, but by the way he scored his runs. Often hindered by ill health, the peaks in his form were generally followed by great troughs, but those have mostly been consigned to the mists of time. Until Bradman came on the scene in the late 1920s, to most Australians, Trumper was the greatest batsman produced by their country. Even now, more than a century after his death, many still consider him in second place.

Immortalised in that glorious 1905 photo by George Beldam, there was far more to Victor Trumper than that. Jack Hobbs described him as 'the most perfect batsman in his scoring methods I have ever seen'. And that came from the man who scored more first-class runs than anyone.

His Test debut came at Trent Bridge in 1899 – by coincidence, W.G. Grace's final Test – and after Trumper had scored a century in the next match at Lord's, Grace appeared demanding a bat from the 'champion of tomorrow' in exchange for one from himself.

It was three years later at Manchester that he really came of age. He reached his century before lunch on the first morning of the Test – the first of only six batsmen to ever achieve that feat.

Runs	Player	Match	Venue	Year
103*	**V.T. Trumper**	**Aus v Eng**	**Manchester**	**1902**
112*	C.G. Macartney	Aus v Eng	Leeds	1926
105*	D.G. Bradman	Aus v Eng	Leeds	1930
108*	Majid Khan	Pak v NZ	Karachi	1976
100*	D.A. Warner	Aus v Pak	Sydney	2017
104*	S. Dhawan	Ind v Afg	Bengaluru	2018

He conquered the wretched weather of 1902 and in all he scored 2,570 runs on that tour of England, including eleven centuries. He was without doubt the finest batsman in the world at that time.

In helpful conditions, he performed some incredible feats of scoring. His unbeaten innings of 185 against England at Sydney in 1903 came in less than four hours, and he mastered the South African googly attack at Adelaide in 1911 to the tune of 214 not out. He scored 98 runs between lunch and tea and then 99 between tea and stumps – both sessions only lasting about ninety minutes each.

Whereas balls faced is strictly speaking a better measure of a batsman's scoring rate, the concept of batting time has been somewhat left behind – especially in the current era of increased strike rates and early finishing Test matches. However, in terms of enjoyment to the spectator, scoring runs in a shorter time will always appear to be more exciting. And that is where Trumper excelled: his overall scoring rate of 40 runs per hour is the fastest in Test history.

Player	Team	Runs	Runs per hour
V.T. Trumper	**Aus**	**3,163**	**40**
S.J. McCabe	Aus	2,748	**38**
F.E. Woolley	Eng	3,283	**38**
C.G. Macartney	Aus	2,131	**37**
D.G. Bradman	Aus	6,996	**37**

His overall Test average of 39.04 does not itself look particularly impressive when compared to those of modern players, but the overall average in Test cricket over that period was 26, making him 50 per cent higher than the average. No one scored more runs than him over the course of his Test career even though he had been weakened by scarlet fever and was never in the best of health later in his life.

Despite that, it was a huge shock when he died at the age of just 37. However, he avoided growing old as a cricketer and suffering the inevitable decline that comes with later years. And he will live forever as shown through the lens of George Beldam.

Hanif Mohammad   international career 1952–69

'For Hanif it was a solemn duty, indeed a vocation, whose fundamental purpose was to ensure that his country was not defeated.' Peter Oborne

An outstanding defensive batsman, who inspired an entire generation of Pakistani batsmen to follow, for a great deal of his life, Hanif Mohammad held the records for both the highest and longest individual innings in first-class cricket. At the time of his death he had to be content with second place in both lists, but his epic 337 in the six-day Test at Bridgetown in 1958 remains by some distance the longest Test innings.

Player	Runs	Mins	Match	Venue	Year
Hanif Mohammad	**337**	**970**	**Pakistan v West Indies**	**Bridgetown**	**1958**
G. Kirsten	275	**878**	South Africa v England	Durban	1999
A.N. Cook	263	**836**	England v Pakistan	Abu Dhabi	2015
S.T. Jayasuriya	340	**799**	Sri Lanka v England	Colombo	1997
L. Hutton	364	**797**	England v Australia	The Oval	1938

Pakistan were asked to follow-on and at the end of day three he was unbeaten on 61. His captain, A.H. Kardar, sent him several notes throughout the duration of his innings, each of which simply said: 'You are our only hope.' He moved on to 161 at the end of the fourth day and 270 at the end of the fifth, before he edged Denis Atkinson to Gerry Alexander 27 runs short of Len Hutton's then Test record of 364. But by that time, the match had been saved.

He had been destined for greatness ever since he became the youngest player to ever score two centuries in a first-class match. That record too has been surpassed – but he was the record holder for more than twenty-five years.

Age	Player	Match	Venue	Year
15y 353d	Farhan Zakhil	Kabul Region v Boost Region	Kabul	2019
17y 8d	Aamer Malik	Lahore City A v Pakistan Railways	Lahore	1980
17y 55d	A.T. Rayudu	Hyderabad v Andhra	Secunderabad	2002
17y 294d	**Hanif Mohammad**	**Pakistanis v North Zone**	**Amritsar**	**1952**

On 11 January 1959, playing for Karachi against Bahawalpur in the Quaid-e-Azam Trophy semi-final, Hanif passed Don Bradman's unbeaten 452 to register the highest first-class score in cricket history. Wazir – his elder brother and captain – had urged him towards the record as he ended the second day not out on 255.

With two balls of the third day left, he was on 498, but the ground scoreboard had not updated and showed his score as 496 instead. He played the ball past point, and after completing the first run, decided to go for the second, intending to keep the strike, but was run out by more than a yard. Bradman sent a congratulatory telegram to Hanif and the two men subsequently met in Australia.

Despite their prolific feats of scoring, Bradman and Hanif thus shared a near-miss. For Bradman it was the iconic average of 99.94, and for Hanif it was the tantalising knowledge that he had fallen one run short of half a thousand.

Pakistan were so dependent on his batting in their early days as a Test nation that by the time he retired he had scored more than a thousand more runs than any other player from his country. Having taken the field with brothers Sadiq and Mushtaq in his last Test match, the dynasty continued with his son Shoaib, who showed he was more than just a chip off the old block by scoring two Test double-centuries. Not content with that, Shoaib's son Shehzar scored a double-century for Karachi Whites in 2018, making them the second three-generation trio to all score first-class double-centuries, after Basil, Damian and Brett D'Oliveira.

Gordon Greenidge   international career 1974–91

'In full flight, he was a glorious sight, and impossible to contain. So awesome was his power, so complete his authority, that once a bombardment was under way not a ball could be bowled to him.' Peter Roebuck

In cricket, perhaps like in no other sport, pairs of names seem to just roll off the tongue, intrinsically linked for all time. Lindwall and Miller, Lillee and Thomson, Ambrose and Walsh, Laker and Lock, Hobbs and Sutcliffe, and Greenidge and Haynes. Even now, nearly thirty years after they last strode to the wicket together for the West Indies, the lattermost are still the most prolific opening partnership in Test cricket.

Partners	Team	Partnerships	Runs	100s
C.G. Greenidge & D.L. Haynes	**WI**	**148**	**6,482**	**16**
M.L. Hayden & J.L. Langer	Aus	113	**5,655**	14
A.N. Cook & A.J. Strauss	Eng	117	**4,711**	12
M.S. Atapattu & S.T. Jayasuriya	SL	118	**4,469**	9
G. Gambhir & V. Sehwag	Ind	87	**4,412**	11

Even though he moved to England from his native Barbados at the age of 14, Gordon Greenidge aligned himself internationally with his country of birth, and thanks to the intervention of John Arlott, signed for Hampshire in 1968 – the same year as Barry Richards. In a parallel universe, he would have sided with England, and could well have ended up opening the England batting with Geoff Boycott for much of the 1970s!

He was seemingly the best of both worlds: an opening batsman who could successfully marry the flair of his birthplace to the defence of his adopted home. Hampshire fans were in for a treat for the majority of the 1970s as they could enjoy the dual delights of Greenidge and Richards opening the batting together, and poor county opening bowlers were to suffer at their hands.

Moving back to the Caribbean to try his luck in the domestic set-up, he was called up to the national squad for the tour of India in late 1974. And on 22 November that year, he made his Test debut at Bengaluru, alongside another player making his first appearance for the West Indies – Viv Richards. While Richards failed to leave his mark on the match as he was dismissed for just 4 and 3, Greenidge became the first West Indian to score a century on Test debut overseas.

Inspired by Tony Greig's 'grovel' remark, the West Indians were in no mood to take any prisoners on their 1976 tour of England. Greenidge struck 134 and 101 at Old Trafford – his first innings coming out of an all-out West Indies total of just 211. He followed up with 115 at Leeds, matching Roy Fredericks stroke for stroke.

If the 1976 tour was triumphant, it was nothing compared to his return eight years later. David Gower must have trusted his bowlers when he declared early on the final day at Lord's, setting the West Indies 342 to win in five and a half hours. In the end, they cantered home with eleven overs to spare, with Greenidge making the highest match-winning score in the fourth innings of any Test.

Score	Player	Match	Venue	Year
214*	**C.G. Greenidge**	**West Indies v England**	**Lord's**	**1984**
182	A.R. Morris	Australia v England	Leeds	1948
173*	D.G. Bradman	Australia v England	Leeds	1948
173*	M.A. Butcher	England v Australia	Leeds	2001
171*	Younis Khan	Pakistan v Sri Lanka	Pallekele	2015

If that wasn't enough, he followed up with 223 at Old Trafford two Tests later to help inspire his team towards their 5-0 series victory.

Understandably, he failed to reach such dizzying heights for the remainder of his career, but his final Test century was also his highest – an innings of 226 on his home ground of Kensington Oval against Australia when just eleven days short of his fortieth birthday. He had only scored 149 runs in his previous ten innings, putting his place in the side in doubt, but his eleven-and-a-half-hour effort ensured he returned to a hero's welcome.

Matthew Hayden   international career 1993–2009

'The best-ever Australian Opener.' Justin Langer

If there was one player who epitomised the all-conquering Australian team of the 2000s, it was Matthew Hayden. Strutting his stuff like a colossus, he looked as if he might have just descended from Mount Olympus to don his whites and baggy green. Likened somewhat unfairly to a playground bully, he was the perfect combination of brain and brawn engineered to succeed in twenty-first-century international cricket.

For a batsman who ended his career with more than 8,000 Test runs at an average of more than 50, he had a slow start. He made his Test debut in 1994 and was then promptly dropped for two and a half years. He returned to the side for three months before being dropped again – this time for three years. Even at that time, he struggled at the highest level, but then came the 2001 tour of India.

Having prepared for the tour on deliberately underprepared dirt tracks, he refined the sweep shot and used it to great effect on the subcontinent. In the three Tests, he struck 119 and 28*, 97 and 67, and 203 and 35, lifting his batting average from a decidedly ordinary 24.36 up to a far more respectable 40.18. There he was to stay – at the top of the Australian batting order for most of the rest of the decade, before an end-of-career slump threatened to push his average below the magical 50 mark.

Whereas openers are often bracketed in a single pair, Hayden managed to form two prolific opening partnerships. In Test cricket it was with Justin Langer, who ironically out-scored Hayden overall in their partnerships together. In white ball cricket it was with Adam Gilchrist, with whom he inspired Australia to World Cup success in both 2003 and 2007, in the latter of which he was the leading run-scorer.

Immortality beckoned when he struck 380 against Zimbabwe at Perth in late 2003 to set a new world Test record. A pushed single to mid off from the bowling of spinner Ray Price in the last over before the tea break on the second day took him past Brian Lara's world record of 375.

It stood for only six months, as Brian Lara reclaimed it with his unbeaten 400. It does remain the second-highest, and the Australian record.

Score	Player	Against	Venue	Year
380	**M.L. Hayden**	**Zimbabwe**	**Perth**	**2003**
335*	D.A. Warner	Pakistan	Adelaide	2019
334*	M.A. Taylor	Pakistan	Peshawar	1998
334	D.G. Bradman	England	Leeds	1930
329*	M.J. Clarke	India	Sydney	2012

Don't have too much sympathy for Hayden: poor Andy Sandham's epic 325 at Kingston in early 1930 stood as the world record for an even shorter time. Bradman's 334 at Leeds came just ninety-nine days later, making Hayden's 185-day reign seem like an eternity!

That innings was an indication of Hayden's desire to 'go big'. Of all the batsmen to have scored at least thirty Test centuries, he has the best conversion rate from 50 to 100.

Player	Team	50+	100+	%
M.L. Hayden	**Aus**	**59**	**30**	**50.84**
Younis Khan	Pak	67	34	**50.74**
J.H. Kallis	SA	103	45	**43.68**
S.M. Gavaskar	Ind	79	34	**43.03**
S.R. Tendulkar	Ind	119	51	**42.85**

Bill Ponsford   **international career 1924–34**

'I liked batting with Bill. He gave me great confidence.' Don Bradman

During the Second World War, Bill Ponsford volunteered to join the Royal Australian Air Force, but was rejected due to his colour blindness. The doctor who examined him was staggered.

'What colour did the new ball look to you?' he asked.

Ponsford replied, 'Red.'

'What colour did it look after it became worn?'

'I never noticed its colour then, only its size.'

Had there been no Don Bradman, it is likely it would be Bill Ponsford who would be remembered today as the Australian with the greatest appetite for phenomenal run-scoring. As it was, his feats of scoring on the true Australian pitches of the 1920s still feature prominently in the record books.

At the age of 13, he was the youngest member of Victoria's Under-18 baseball team. John McGraw – the manager of the New York Giants at the time – saw him in action and tried to persuade Ponsford's parents to send him to America. However, he elected to stay, and began his senior career as a catcher for Fitzroy before going on to represent Victoria. Had they accepted McGraw's offer, he could have ended up a contemporary of Babe Ruth, Lou Gehrig and Hack Wilson, and the cricket record books would have looked somewhat different.

Ponsford wielded a heavy bat, which was fondly termed 'Big Bertha' due to its 2lb 10oz weight. Playing in just his third first-class game, he batted for eight hours to score 429 for Victoria against Tasmania at Melbourne in 1923 and set a new record individual score. In December 1927, he faced Queensland and became the only batsman in the last 200 years to better his own world record, scoring 437.

Score	Player	Match	Venue	Year
78	J. Small snr	Hampshire v England	Hambledon	1772
88	W. Yalden	Surrey v Hampshire	Hambledon	1773
95	R. Miller	Kent v Hampshire	Sevenoaks	1774
138	J. Small snr	Hampshire v Surrey	Hambledon	1775
167	J. Aylward	Hampshire v England	Sevenoaks	1777
278	W. Ward	MCC v Norfolk	Lord's	1820

344	W.G. Grace	Gentlemen of MCC v Kent	Canterbury	1876
424	A.C. MacLaren	Lancashire v Somerset	Taunton	1895
429	**W.H. Ponsford**	**Victoria v Tasmania**	**Melbourne**	**1923**
437	**W.H. Ponsford**	**Victoria v Queensland**	**Melbourne**	**1927**
452*	D.G. Bradman	New South Wales v Queensland	Sydney	1930
499	Hanif Mohammad	Karachi v Bahawalpur	Karachi – KP	1959
501*	B.C. Lara	Warwickshire v Durham	Birmingham	1994

He then followed it up with 202 against New South Wales later that month, and as 1928 dawned, he hit 336 against South Australia to total 1,013 runs in four innings.

He confounded those who thought he could only perform in State cricket by scoring centuries in each of his first two Tests – against England in the 1924/25 Ashes series. However, he struggled later in his career against the pace of Harold Larwood, who broke his hand in the 1928/29 series and held him to an average of just 23.50 in the 'Bodyline' series four years later.

By the time the England tour of 1930 took place, Ponsford had been replaced as the number one run machine by Don Bradman, but he signed off from international cricket in the grandest of styles, with 181 at Leeds before striking 266 at The Oval in 1934, the second-highest score by anyone in their final Test.

Score	Player	Match	Venue	Year
325	A. Sandham	England v West Indies	Kingston	1930
266	**W.H. Ponsford**	**Australia v England**	**The Oval**	**1934**
258	S.M. Nurse	West Indies v New Zealand	Christchurch	1969
206	P.A. de Silva	Sri Lanka v Bangladesh	Colombo – PSS	2002
201*	J.N. Gillespie	Australia v Bangladesh	Chittagong	2006

Saeed Anwar   international career 1989–2003

'As far as talent is concerned, Saeed Anwar is not far behind Lara and Tendulkar.'
Imran Khan

Like Graham Gooch before him, Saeed Anwar's Test career started with a 'pair', against the West Indies at Faisalabad. As pairs go, it wasn't a bad one – inflicted by Curtly Ambrose and Ian Bishop – but it meant exile from the Test team for more than three years.

The fact that he played cricket at all was more through luck than judgement. He grew up in Iran playing football, after his father obtained an engineering job there. However, when another job took him to Saudi Arabia, Anwar returned to Karachi to live with his grandparents.

He carefully honed his technique in a garage, repeatedly facing the bowling of a friend from the area who covered a tennis ball with tape. That friend was Rashid Latif, and the two would go on to play sixteen Tests for Pakistan together.

By the time he had a second chance of Test cricket he had already become prolific in ODI cricket, having notched up six centuries in his first forty-one matches. He was instrumental in giving Pakistan thrilling starts in the shorter form of the game, the speed of his scoring more reliant on grace and elegance than brute force. He had also acquired a degree in Computer Systems Engineering from NED University, and but for his cricket, he would probably have ended up studying for a Masters in the United States, like so many of his former student colleagues.

As with so many players, his strength could also be his weakness. For every scything cut played against a bowler offering him even a modicum of room outside his off stump, there was the occasional casual waft that invariably ended in the hands of a gully fielder.

For thirteen years, Viv Richards' unbeaten innings of 189 made against England at Old Trafford in 1984 had stood as the world record score in ODI cricket. However, on 21 May 1997, the stars aligned for Anwar in Chennai against India and he struck 194 from 146 deliveries, with a little bit of help from Shahid Afridi, who acted as his runner from the eighteenth over onwards. Ironically, the man who finally dismissed him that day – Sachin Tendulkar – would himself eclipse Anwar's record with the first ODI double-century some thirteen years later.

Score	Player	Match	Venue	Date
82	J.H. Edrich	England v Australia	Melbourne	Jan 1971
103	D.L. Amiss	England v Australia	Manchester	Aug 1972
105	R.C. Fredericks	West Indies v England	The Oval	Sep 1973
116*	D. Lloyd	England v Pakistan	Nottingham	Aug 1974

171*	G.M. Turner	New Zealand v East Africa	Birmingham	Jun 1975
175*	Kapil Dev	India v Zimbabwe	Tunbridge Wells	Jun 1983
189*	I.V.A. Richards	West Indies v England	Manchester	May 1984
194	**Saeed Anwar**	**Pakistan v India**	**Chennai**	**May 1997**
194*	C.K. Coventry	Zimbabwe v Bangladesh	Bulawayo	Aug 2009
200*	S.R. Tendulkar	India v South Africa	Gwalior	Feb 2010
219	V. Sehwag	India v West Indies	Indore – TG	Dec 2011
264	R.G. Sharma	India v Sri Lanka	Kolkata	Nov 2014

The highlight of his Test career also came against India, this time in the first match of the Asian Test Championship at Kolkata in February 1999. An estimated crowd of 465,000 saw Pakistan beat India by 46 runs in a match marred by crowd trouble but highlighted by one of the all-time great Test innings.

India had grabbed a first-innings lead of 38 but Anwar carried his bat through Pakistan's second innings of 316, scoring an unbeaten 188. It meant that the hosts needed 279 to win. The openers put on a century partnership, but the run-out of Sachin Tendulkar precipitated a collapse, and Pakistan ended up victorious. It remains the highest individual score for any Pakistan batsman carrying his bat through a Test innings.

Player	Score	Total	Against	Venue	Year
Saeed Anwar	**188***	**316**	**India**	**Calcutta**	**1999**
Mudassar Nazar	**152***	323	India	Lahore	1983
Nazar Mohammad	**124***	331	India	Lucknow – U	1952
Imran Farhat	**117***	223	New Zealand	Napier	2009

Glenn Turner   international career 1969–83

'Unswervingly single-minded in his pursuit of runs and unashamedly ambitious.'
Christopher Martin-Jenkins

1968 was a big year around the world for many reasons. It saw the assassinations of Robert Kennedy and Martin Luther King Jr, the Prague Spring in Czechoslovakia, the start of the Tet Offensive in Vietnam, and the Paris riots. It was no less eventful on the sports field, with Manchester United winning the European Cup and Bob Beamon ruining the Mexico City Olympic Long Jump final by leaping a stupendous 8.90 metres with his first jump. It was also the year Glenn Turner came to Worcestershire – and he came by sea!

Desperate to make an impression, he struggled at the start, only scoring 29 runs from his first six innings. However, he began to acclimatise to the English conditions, and eventually passed a thousand runs, a feat he would repeat thirteen times for the county.

New Zealand had a somewhat tortuous start to their Test history and by the time Turner made his Test debut in February 1969, they had won just four of their eighty-three matches to date. They had great cricketers before Turner; Bert Sutcliffe averaged more than 40 but was winless in his forty-two Tests. What they needed was someone who could lift them and help bring about victories, and they found that person in Turner.

In Turner's favour was an insatiable appetite for scoring runs. This was never more in evidence than on the 1971/72 tour of the Caribbean. Having warmed up for the Test series with an innings of 202 against the West Indies Board President's XI, in the First Test he became just the fourth player to carry his bat through a complete Test innings on two occasions, scoring 223 not out – then the highest score by anyone performing the feat.

Another warm-up game before the fourth Test brought another double-century, this time an innings of 259 against Guyana. Astonishingly, he was at it again the following week, on the same ground, scoring an identical 259 as part of an opening partnership of 387 with Terry Jarvis. That partnership remains the longest in Test history in terms of balls faced.

Balls	Runs	Wkt	Partners	Match	Venue	Year
1,152	387	1	**G.M. Turner & T.W. Jarvis**	**NZ v WI**	**Georgetown**	**1972**
1,146	411	4	P.B.H. May & M.C. Cowdrey	Eng v WI	Birmingham	1957
1,110	576	2	S.T. Jayasuriya & R.S. Mahanama	SL v Ind	Colombo	1997

Turner's prodigious feats of run-scoring continued unabated in England, where in 1973 he became the first batsman since the Second World War to score a thousand runs before the end of May. The following winter at Christchurch, he became the first New Zealand batsman to score two centuries in a Test as he inspired his country's first Test victory over Australia.

He scored two centuries in the 1975 World Cup, the first an unbeaten 171 against East Africa, which remained the ODI record for eight years until Kapil Dev's 1983 tour de force at Tunbridge Wells.

His career with Worcestershire culminated with his hundredth first-class century, which uniquely he converted into a triple century against Warwickshire, celebrating on the field with a gin and tonic! But of all his 103 first-class centuries, probably the most famous remains his unbeaten 141 against Glamorgan at Swansea. Nothing so unusual about that, but none of his teammates were able to score more than 7 runs each. That performance still ranks as the highest percentage of a team total in any completed innings.

%	Runs	Total	Player	Match	Venue	Year
83.43	**141**	**169**	**G.M. Turner**	**Worcestershire v Glamorgan**	**Swansea**	**1977**
81.56	230	282	G. Snyman	Namibia v Kenya	Sharjah	2008
80.00	172	215	Khalid Latif	Port Qasim Authority v United Bank Ltd.	Islamabad	2015
79.84	309	387	V.S. Hazare	The Rest v Hindus	Mumbai	1943
79.25	126	159	W.G. Grace	United South of England v United North of England	Hull	1876

Chapter 2
Middle-Order Batsmen

Donald Bradman   **international career 1928–48**

'He is a text-book of batting come to life with never a misprint or erratum.' J.M. Kilburn

Out of the Great Depression stepped a new national hero – Don Bradman – who set records for high scoring that had only been dreamed of. After setting the world alight on the 1930 tour of England, in which he scored 974 runs in the Tests – a record that still stands – the Bodyline plan was devised to stop him scoring. It worked to some extent as he averaged a 'mere' 56. It was back to normal on the 1934 tour of England though, and the Ashes were not surrendered again until after his retirement.

Even now, more than seventy years after his final Test, Bradman's batting average of 99.94 looks like a misprint. Not only is it probably the most famous number in a sport obsessed by numbers, but it is nearly 40 runs better than the next batsman on the list to have batted more than twenty times in Test cricket. It could be said that it is the most remarkable sporting outlier of them all.

Player	Team	Innings	Runs	Avge
D.G. Bradman	**Aus**	**80**	**6,996**	**99.94**
M. Labuschagne	Aus	23	1,459	**63.43**
S.P.D. Smith	Aus	131	7,227	**62.84**
A.C. Voges	Aus	31	1,485	**61.87**
R.G. Pollock	SA	41	2,256	**60.97**

Back in 1968, Bob Beamon bypassed the 28 feet mark and leaped 29 feet 2½ inches to win gold in the Mexico Olympics. That record was considered unbreakable, but one night in Tokyo in 1991, Mike Powell did just that, and Powell's record has now lasted longer than Beamon's did.

However, Bradman's figures have survived the test of time. Some detractors would say that he gorged on flat wickets, timeless Tests and weakened bowling attacks. But these runs were scored on uncovered wickets with only a cap to protect him against the onslaught from the opposition bowlers. Added to that, he scored more quickly than most of his contemporaries, and still holds the record for the most runs in a day's play in Test cricket.

Player	Runs	Match	Venue	Year
D.G. Bradman	**309**	**Australia v England**	**Leeds**	**1930**
W.R. Hammond	**295**	England v New Zealand	Auckland	1933
V. Sehwag	**284**	India v Sri Lanka	Mumbai (BS)	2009
D.C.S. Compton	**273**	England v Pakistan	Nottingham	1954
D.G. Bradman	**271**	Australia v England	Leeds	1934

At the end of the first day of the Leeds Test in 1934, Bradman declined an invitation to dinner from writer Neville Cardus, saying that he wanted an early night because the team needed him to make a double-century. Cardus pointed out that his previous innings on the ground was 334, and the law of averages was against another such score. Bradman told Cardus, 'I don't believe in the law of averages,' and subsequently scored 304.

Every cricket fan is aware of how Bradman was dismissed for a duck in his final innings at The Oval in 1948, just 4 runs short of a batting average of a hundred. He may have batted again in the match – possibly unlikely as he strode to the crease with his side 117-1, having already dismissed England for just 52. But it is those tantalising 4 runs he didn't score – just 4 runs out of a career of nearly twenty years and nearly 200 hours at the crease – that are possibly the first to be discussed whenever he is mentioned.

He probably signed more autographs than any player in history and by the time he died, was possibly the most famous and revered Australian of them all.

Viv Richards   international career 1974–91

'He bats with the passionate intensity of a murderer rather than the cool rationality of an assassin.' Peter Roebuck

From the moment he swaggered out of the pavilion, gum-chewing and arm-swinging, the spectators knew they were in the presence of greatness. Perhaps no other player – save perhaps his long-time friend and now fellow knight, Ian Botham – possessed such self-belief. In addition to that, he had the talent to instil that self-belief in all those around him, lifting otherwise average sides to greatness.

Before the era of massive bats, Richards was an innovator. No one hit the ball harder, and to this day, no one has managed to emulate his trademark whip through midwicket from a delivery outside off stump.

He learned his craft by rolling his own pitch in Antigua, where he tried to counter the irregular bounce by hitting across the line. Along with another promising player from his island – Andy Roberts – he was sent to Alf Gover's Cricket School in 1972, where fortunately his technique remained essentially unaltered. When he was spotted by Somerset's vice-chairman, he was offered the chance to play in the West Country and lifted the county to five trophies.

International honours came late in 1974 but he struggled in his first Test at Bengaluru, making just 4 and 3 before being dismissed by Chandrasekhar in each innings. He put things right in spectacular fashion in the next match, striking an unbeaten 192, which included six sixes.

He pretty much single-handedly put Antigua on the map. Sugar used to be their major crop, but he soon became their major export, lighting up cricket grounds all over the world. His first major contribution on the international stage was in the 1975 World Cup, when he ran out three Australians in the final. In the following year he entered the realms of cricketing immortals.

Clive Lloyd's team made a mockery of Tony Greig's promise to make them 'grovel' beforehand, and that was just the start. Richards struck 232 at Trent Bridge, 135 at Old Trafford and 291 at The Oval, totalling 1,710 runs in all Test cricket that year – setting a record that stood for thirty years.

Player	Team	Year	Matches	**Runs**	Avge
Mohammad Yousuf	Pak	2006	11	**1,788**	99.33
I.V.A. Richards	**WI**	**1976**	**11**	**1,710**	**90.00**
G.C. Smith	SA	2008	15	**1,656**	72.00
M.J. Clarke	Aus	2012	11	**1,595**	106.33
S.R. Tendulkar	Ind	2010	14	**1,562**	78.10

In One Day International cricket he was arguably even more successful. The West Indies retained the World Cup trophy in 1979 with a Richards masterclass in the final against England. Then, in 1984, he played what is still considered to be the greatest of all ODI innings. Against England at Old Trafford, his side were deep in trouble at 102-7 in the twenty-sixth over. Eldine Baptiste helped him add 59 for the eighth wicket, but as Michael Holding strode to the crease, the score was 166-9, with Richards 96 not out.

What followed was a stunning display of hitting, with Holding lucky enough to have the best seat in the house. Botham, Pringle, Willis and Foster all suffered as the final wicket partnership swelled to an unbeaten 106, Holding's share of which was 12. Richards ended with 189 not out – a world record at the time – and that effort helped him on his way to the highest ICC batting rating in ODI cricket history.

Player	Team	Year	Points
I.V.A. Richards	WI	1985	935
Zaheer Abbas	Pak	1983	931
G.S. Chappell	Aus	1981	921
D.I. Gower	Eng	1983	919
D.M. Jones	Aus	1991	918
V. Kohli	Ind	2018	911

Richards took over as captain when Clive Lloyd retired, and led the team in a further fifty Tests without ever losing a single series. He was knighted in 1999, but to many, he was always the uncrowned King of Antigua.

Sachin Tendulkar **international career 1989–2013**

'He has been in form longer than some of our guys have been alive.' Daniel Vettori

It wasn't just about the runs – or the centuries. It was about dealing with the weight of a billion fans on your shoulders every time you walked out to bat. And Sachin Tendulkar dealt with that pressure and came out the other end as possibly the most adored cricketer in the game's history.

To enjoy such a long career, it helped to start young, and he scored an unbeaten century on his first-class debut at the age of just 15. He had already been in the headlines, as he had shared in an unbroken partnership of 664 with Vinod Kambli for Shardashram Vidyamandir against St Xavier's High School in the Harris Shield semi-final in 1988. Whereas Kambli shone brightly before fading quickly, Tendulkar was in for the long run, ending as the leading run-scorer in all international cricket.

Player	Team	Runs
S.R. Tendulkar	Ind	34,357
K.C. Sangakkara	SL	28,016
R.T. Ponting	Aus	27,483
D.P.M.D. Jayawardene	SL	25,957
J.H. Kallis	SA	25,534

A Test debut followed in 1989 and he was dismissed by fellow debutant Waqar Younis in his first Test innings. A Graham Gooch-inspired England won the series the following year, but at Old Trafford, a star was born. With his team batting last, he stroked an unbeaten 119 – the first of his record 100 international centuries. In 1992, he became the youngest player to score a Test century in Australia and left an indelible mark on the world game.

Before he arrived on the scene, India had won just forty-three Tests in their first fifty-seven years as a Test nation. By the time he left the international arena, they had managed to win seventy-two of his record 200 Tests. His first ODI century didn't arrive until his seventy-ninth match but he soon made up for lost time, and in 2010 he became the first man to hit a double-century in Limited Overs International cricket.

He reached his peak in the late 1990s, when none of the great bowlers at the time could say they had the better of him. Indian audiences were treated to a seemingly never-ending succession of great innings flowing from his bat, beamed into their houses once the BCCI had awoken to the tremendous benefit of selling television rights. Tendulkar became the biggest reason that cricket moved from being an enjoyable pastime to a national obsession.

After a relative struggle through 2005 and 2006, when his lower back and tennis elbow injuries started to take their toll, he had a remarkable second wind, striking thirteen more Test centuries in three years to move back up to top spot in the ICC's Test batting rankings. That second coming culminated in India's World Cup triumph on home soil in 2011, a tournament in which Tendulkar was his team's leading run-scorer.

With no obvious technical weaknesses, his game was built on balance and precision, and an uncanny ability to play the ball later than most of his peers. His elevation to opening the batting in limited-overs cricket was a revelation, and he and Sourav Ganguly formed the most productive partnership ever seen in ODI cricket.

Partners	Team	Partnerships	Runs	100s
S.R. Tendulkar & S.C. Ganguly	**Ind**	**176**	**8,228**	**26**
D.P.M.D. Jayawardene & K.C. Sangakkara	SL	150	**5,992**	15
T.M. Dilshan & K.C. Sangakkara	SL	108	**5,475**	20
S.T. Jayasuriya & M.S. Atapattu	SL	144	**5,462**	14
M.L. Hayden & A.C. Gilchrist	Aus	117	**5,409**	16

Tendulkar's international career ended pretty much exactly twenty-four years after it started – the fifth-longest of all time. And what better way to end than in a Test victory on his home ground?

Brian Lara   international career 1990–2007

'He is charming, vulnerable, endearing, moody, impossible to work out at times and endlessly fascinating.' Steve Waugh

If one thing can be said about Brian Lara it is that his appetite for runs was unmatched throughout his career. He not only broke Garry Sobers' long-standing Test record score of 365 but, having lost it to Matthew Hayden, regained it several months later with an unbeaten innings of 400 against England at Antigua.

Score	Player	Match	Venue	Year
400*	**B.C. Lara**	**West Indies v England**	**St John's**	**2004**
380	M.L. Hayden	Australia v Zimbabwe	Perth	2003
375	**B.C. Lara**	**West Indies v England**	**St John's**	**1994**
374	D.P.M.D. Jayawardene	Sri Lanka v South Africa	Colombo – SSC	2006
365*	G.S. Sobers	West Indies v Pakistan	Kingston	1958

There was also his unbeaten 501 against Durham when playing for Warwickshire in the 1994 county season – which remains a record in all first-class cricket. That innings was the culmination of an incredible run of scoring in which he became the first batsman to score seven centuries in eight innings.

Score	Player	Match	Venue	Year
501*	**B.C. Lara**	**Warwickshire v Durham**	**Birmingham**	**1994**
499	Hanif Mohammad	Karachi v Bahawalpur	Karachi	1959
452*	D.G. Bradman	NSW v Queensland	Sydney	1930
443*	B.B. Nimbalkar	Maharashtra v Kathiawar	Pune	1948
437	W.H. Ponsford	Victoria v Queensland	Melbourne	1927

It wasn't just the number of runs he scored, but the way he scored them that enthralled crowds around the world. Equally comfortable against pace and spin, his high backlift coupled with a full flourish of the bat brought great flamboyance to the crease.

He received his first bat at the age of just 3, and his formal coaching started three years later at Harvard Club in Port of Spain. In his early years he was a good enough footballer to make it into the national youth squad, where he struck up a long-lasting friendship with Dwight Yorke, who followed a different path to sporting greatness.

He was fortunate enough to be mentored by the former West Indies opening batsman Joey Carew, and he made a total of 745 runs at an average of 126.16

for his school at the age of 14. That performance propelled him into the sights of the Trinidad selectors, and he went on to represent the West Indies in the 1988 Under-19 World Cup in Australia.

He didn't set the world alight in that competition but burst onto the international scene with an innings of 277 against Australia at Sydney in 1993. However, for all his tall scoring, possibly his finest innings was an unbeaten 153 against Australia at Barbados in March 1999, which helped the home side to a one-wicket victory.

His time in charge of the national side was not a particularly happy one, with just ten victories and twenty-six defeats coming in his forty-seven Tests in charge. His own form started to suffer too, with ducks in three successive Tests in England in 2000. However, a suggestion from Sobers that he alter his backlift brought him back into record-breaking form.

In November 2001, he struck 221 and 130 against a rampant Muralitharan at Colombo – the most runs ever scored in a losing cause in a Test. Two more double centuries followed in 2003, and the following year he captained the West Indies to victory in the ICC Champions Trophy in England.

Unlike his predecessors in the West Indian middle order, he was not blessed with a world-beating team around him. Subsequently, only Bradman and Headley scored more than Lara's 18.95 per cent of their team's runs when they were in the team. Despite the paucity of the West Indian side of the 1990s, there is no denying the fact that he was the biggest box office draw in cricket throughout that decade.

Wally Hammond   international career 1927–47

'For Hammond was majesty and power; Hammond was grace, beauty and courage. One glorious cover drive from him and I would be content.' Margaret Hughes

Born in Dover, Wally Hammond had a multicultural upbringing, moving first to Hong Kong at the age of 5, and then to Malta when he was 11, where he played his first cricket. After returning to England he attended Cirencester Grammar School, where his love affair with the county of Gloucestershire started. Perhaps sensing they might have missed out on a good 'un, Kent asked him to play for them on account of his birth qualification, but he refused and chose to stay in the West Country.

Had he never picked up a bat he would have been considered a pretty decent cricketer. With 732 first-class wickets at 30 apiece and a best bowling of 9-23, he was a more than useful third seamer. He was peerless in the slips and ended with more than 800 catches … and then there was his batting!

Having first toured with England in the 1925/26 winter to the Caribbean, serious illness put his Test debut back until December 1927, seven months after he had become just the second of the three batsmen to score a thousand runs in the month of May.

Player	Year	Days	Innings
W.G. Grace	1895	22	10
W.R. Hammond	**1927**	**22**	**13**
C. Hallows	1928	27	11

Hammond's first eight Tests brought four half-centuries, but then came the 1928/29 Ashes series in Australia, when the floodgates opened. He struck 251 at Sydney, 200 at Melbourne and a double of 119 not out and 177 at Adelaide, taking over the mantle as England's premier batsman from Jack Hobbs. He totalled 905 runs in the series, which remains a record for any England batsman.

Player	Against	Season	Runs
W.R. Hammond	**Australia**	**1928/29**	**905**
A.N. Cook	Australia	2010/11	**766**
D.C.S. Compton	South Africa	1947	**753**
G.A. Gooch	India	1990	**752**
H. Sutcliffe	Australia	1924/25	**734**

In what was seen as a 'competition within a competition', Hammond drew first blood in his battle with the Australian supremo, Bradman. In total, the two master batsmen faced each other in thirty-one Tests, but Hammond was unsuccessful in his two Ashes series as captain.

He was the first batsman to reach 6,000 and then 7,000 Test runs and his eventual aggregate remained a record until Colin Cowdrey broke it more than twenty years later. Hammond also set a Test record with an unbeaten innings of 336 against New Zealand at Auckland in 1933.

In the Second World War, he joined the RAF and was posted to Cairo, but did not see active service. He played quite a bit of cricket in Africa, but once the war was over, he was not the same player. The Ashes series of 1946/47 was a disaster, and he was never to play for England again after that tour.

In domestic cricket he was peerless, topping the domestic averages for eight successive summers – a record that still stands. His cover drive is still perhaps the most famous stroke in the game's history and he uniquely captained both Players and Gentlemen in the annual fixture at Lord's. As his obituary in Wisden summed him up: 'he was, unchallengeably, one of the cricketing immortals'.

Denis Compton   **international career 1937–57**

'There were no rations in an innings by Compton.' Neville Cardus

The Second World War had been won, but the mood was still overcast. This was the time of rationing and constant reminders of the madness left the English pessimistic. Out of this backdrop was launched Denis Compton – the kind of player everyone wanted to be.

Born in North West London, he grew up knowing that the Number 13 bus went to Lord's. In fact, it still does. He showed immediate talent and was playing for his school's First XI at the tender age of 10. A century for London Elementary Schools at Lord's at the age of 14 impressed so many that he was signed up to join the Lord's groundstaff as soon as he left school. His pen was busy that year, for he also signed on the dotted line up the road for Arsenal.

He was just 21 years old when the war put a premature end to his bright start. He was sent to India to help train men in preparation for the battles against Japan, and while there he managed to find time to play some first-class cricket, scoring 249 not out in the Ranji Trophy final in March 1945. Frequently he forgot to bring his kit to matches and had to borrow some from a teammate. That just added to the allure.

After the war he emerged as a dashing, debonair hero of the nation. It was as if he had been sent to give joy to a morose country in need of a shining light. In 1947, runs flowed like never before to the tune of 3,806 in first-class cricket, with eighteen centuries, both records that will never be surpassed.

Player	Year	Runs
D.C.S. Compton	1947	3,806
W.J. Edrich	1947	3,539
T.W. Hayward	1906	3,518
L. Hutton	1949	3,429
F.E. Woolley	1928	3,352

Compton was possibly the first 'film star' cricketer, with looks to match his talent on the field. Not just the cricket field, however, as he and his brother Leslie played football for Arsenal and were good enough to win the 1950 FA Cup together.

As a batsman he had all the strokes, and memorably played his famous sweep shot to regain the Ashes at The Oval in 1953 after they had been in Australian hands for nineteen years. The following year, he struck his highest Test score of 278 against Pakistan at Trent Bridge, which included 173 runs between lunch and tea on the second day – still the record for the most runs by an individual in a single session of play in a Test.

Runs	Player	Match	Venue	Year	Session
173	**D.C.S. Compton**	**England v Pakistan**	**Nottingham**	**1954**	**D2 S2**
150	W.R. Hammond	England v New Zealand	Auckland	1933	D2 S2
140	I.D.S. Smith	New Zealand v India	Auckland	1990	D1 S3
139	N.J. Astle	New Zealand v England	Christchurch	2002	D4 S3
133	V.T. Trumper	Australia v South Africa	Melbourne	1911	D3 S3

In 2002, the world waited for David Beckham's broken metatarsal to heal, but for Denis Compton there was always the spectre of his knee. First injured in a collision with Charlton's goalkeeper, Sid Hobbins, in 1938, he had numerous operations, which finally meant the removal of the kneecap. His duels with Ray Lindwall and Keith Miller entered cricket legend, as did his dubious running between the wickets, which culminated in his running out Leslie in his brother's benefit match. Trevor Bailey stated that 'a call for a run from Compton should be treated as no more than a basis for negotiation'.

He could bowl, too – taking 622 first-class wickets with his left-arm wrist-spin bowling. He will be remembered as a trendsetter, employing the first sports agent – Bagenal Harvey – to help seal a famous contract with Brylcreem. That is how he is remembered – batting at Lord's, hair slicked back, scoring yet another century.

George Headley   **international career 1930–54**

'The yardstick against whom all other West Indian batsmen are measured.'
Michael Manley

The ultimate comparison for any batsman is to Donald Bradman. It says something that in his day, George Headley was known as the 'Black Bradman'. Perhaps apocryphally, it is also said that in the 1930s, Bradman was occasionally referred to as the 'White Headley'! Whether true or not, in a decade of high scoring, Headley was one of the leading lights and the first great batsman produced by the West Indies. Of all batsmen who have batted at least a hundred times in first-class cricket, only two have posted a higher average.

Player	Runs	Avge
D.G. Bradman	28,067	**95.14**
V.M. Merchant	13,470	**71.64**
G.A. Headley	**9,921**	69.86
A.K. Sharma	10,120	**67.46**
W.H. Ponsford	13,819	**65.18**

Relatively small, Headley struck the ball incredibly hard and always appeared to time it perfectly. He was particularly a master of back-foot play, a talent that enabled him to score equally freely in England, Australia and the Caribbean.

Born in Panama, where his father had been helping to build the famous canal, he was taken to Jamaica at the age of 10 to improve his English. Once there, he fell in love with cricket at school, displayed rare promise and made his first-class debut at the age of 18 against Lionel Tennyson's touring side. In his second match, he scored 211, but it still wasn't enough to earn a berth on the West Indies first tour of England in 1928.

He made up for lost time when England travelled to the Caribbean eighteen months later, making a total of 703 runs in the Tests. He scored 176 on his Test debut at Barbados, and added twin centuries at Guyana before striking 223 at Jamaica. A legend had been born and all this had been achieved before a domestic competition between the islands had started, and with a different captain for each Test.

The following year, Australia were mastered at Brisbane and Sydney before Lionel — now Lord — Tennyson tried again with a tour in early 1932. Their first match was a sobering occasion, as Headley scored an unbeaten 344 for Jamaica at Melbourne Park, adding an unbroken 487 runs for the sixth wicket with Clarence Passailaigue.

Jamaica won all three of those matches, and Headley toured England for the first time in 1933, striking 169 not out at Old Trafford. He went even better in the return series in the Caribbean in 1935, when he hit an unbeaten 270 in the Jamaica Test, which remained a West Indies record for twenty-three years.

Cricket was sporadic for the West Indies and so Headley's next series was the 1939 tour of England – the final international action before the Second World War. In a match in which only one of his teammates passed 30 in either innings, he became the only batsman to score two centuries in a Test against England on two separate occasions, and the first batsman to ever score two centuries in a Lord's Test.

Player	Scores	Match	Year
G.A. Headley	**106 & 107**	**West Indies v England**	**1939**
G.A. Gooch	**333 & 123**	England v India	1990
M.P. Vaughan	**103 & 101***	England v West Indies	2004

He was not the same when hostilities ceased, and he made two Test appearances in 1948 before signing off aged 45 against England on his home patch of Jamaica in 1954, ending with a Test average of more than 60.

Frank Worrell   international career 1948–63

'It was impossible to set a field to him. Place the fieldsmen straight and he beat them on the wide. Place them wide and he would beat them straight.' Norman Yardley

If ever a player's off-field persona matched his on-field grace and style, that man was Frank Worrell. When his team lost the memorable 1960/61 Test series in Australia, half a million fans lined the streets of Melbourne to bid them farewell. Despite dying early, at the age of 42, and being awarded a memorial service at Westminster Abbey, his name lives on for fans and in the name of the trophy competed for by Australia and the West Indies in Test cricket.

Worrell was the oldest of the 'three Ws' (the others being Clyde Walcott and Everton Weekes) – all born within seventeen months and one mile of each other, and all within walking distance of the Kensington Oval. It is also believed that all three were delivered by the same midwife. He was born to working-class parents and was admitted to Combermere School at the age of 12. He flourished under the watchful eye of Derek Sealy, who had played eleven pre-war Tests for the West Indies, and Worrell first appeared for the school's First XI as a specialist left-arm spinner, taking a seven-wicket haul against Harrison College.

By the time he left school, he was considered the premier left-arm spinner in the country, but his batting soon developed once he was playing for his native Barbados. At the age of 19 he shared an unbroken partnership of 502 with John Goddard, and two years later he added 574 without being separated from Walcott. To this day, only one other batsman has played a part in two partnerships of more than 500 runs.

Player	500+ partnerships
F.M.M. Worrell	2
R.A. Jadeja	2

As a batsman he was graceful, stroking the ball with perfect timing. He had the air of an artist and not only could he play every stroke in the book, he did so without ever appearing to be hurried.

A year spent in the Lancashire League was enough to cement his mastery of English conditions as he struck 261 in the 1950 Nottingham Test – the series in which the three Ws first really hit the headlines as a triple threat. He added 138 at The Oval, topping the batting averages with a total of 539 runs at 89.83. He was back in England in 1957 and scored an unbeaten 191 at Trent Bridge, becoming the first West Indian to carry his bat through a completed Test innings.

Player	Score	Total	Against	Venue	Year
F.M.M. Worrell	**191***	**372**	**England**	**Nottingham**	**1957**
C.C. Hunte	60*	131	Australia	Port of Spain	1965
D.L. Haynes	88*	211	Pakistan	Karachi	1986
D.L. Haynes	75*	176	England	The Oval	1991
D.L. Haynes	143*	382	Pakistan	Port of Spain	1993
C.H. Gayle	165*	317	Australia	Adelaide	2009
K.C. Brathwaite	142*	337	Pakistan	Sharjah	2016

Worrell's bowling also made the headlines as he took 7-70 in the next Test at Leeds. Once the tour was over, he stayed behind to take a degree in Economics at the University of Manchester. When England toured in 1960, he scored 197 not out at Bridgetown and at the end of the season he was appointed captain.

As leader he managed to unite the rivalries between the islands and that 1960/61 tour of Australia was a watershed. The series ended in a 2-1 victory for the hosts, but the tied Test at Brisbane is still regarded as possibly the greatest match of all time. On India's tour of the West Indies in 1962, Nari Contractor was struck on the head by Charlie Griffith in the game against Barbados and suffered a fractured skull. Worrell was the first to donate blood, which helped save Contractor's life. That action is commemorated annually as 'Frank Worrell Day' in India, when a blood donation drive is held.

His final triumph was the 3-1 victory in England in 1963, when he was not at his best, and he retired after the tour but still contributed to West Indies cricket as both manager and selector.

K.S. Ranjitsinhji   international career 1896–1902

'If the supreme art is to achieve the maximum result with the minimum expenditure of effort, the Jam Sahib, as a batsman, is in a class by himself.' A.G. Gardiner

In recent days we have had the 'Dilscoop' and the 'Helicopter Shot' but there have been few men throughout cricket history to have been able to claim they invented a shot. Indian Prince Ranji was one of those men. His leg glance went against the age-old custom of hitting back in the direction from where the bowling came from. He invented new angles on both sides of the wicket as his late cut was equally deft.

He was related to the ruling family of the state of Nawanagar in Western India through his grandfather, and he was educated at Rajkumar College in Rajkot, a finishing school for young princes. He flourished there, winning prizes for English speaking and gymnastics, and his sporting prowess started to emerge, under the tutelage of the principal there, Chester Macnaghten. He captained the school cricket team for five years before opportunity came knocking at the age of 16.

He was one of three princes chosen to travel to England for further education and he attended Cambridge University, where he made more headlines as the owner of the first motor car in the city than he did for any academic excellence! At the time he did not give any impression of becoming a future star but started to refine his technique, helped by employing some of the greatest coaches in the game to help him on his way.

He started representing Trinity College and was eventually selected for the full Cambridge University side. After failing to graduate and under pressure to return to India, he accepted an invitation to play for Sussex in 1895. His first match for the county was against MCC at Lord's and he struck 77 not out and 150, and ended the season with an aggregate of 1,775 runs at an average of nearly 50. But there was better to come.

The year 1896 will always be etched in sports fans' minds as the first year of the Modern Olympic Games. But while Pierre de Coubertin's Athens show took some of the headlines, Manchester saw another when Ranji made his Test debut against the Australians. Having made 62 in the first innings, he struck twenty-three boundaries in a memorable unbeaten 154 second time around, the highest score by an England batsman on debut in England.

Score	Player	Against	Venue	Year
154*	**K.S. Ranjitsinhji**	**Australia**	**Manchester**	**1896**
152	W.G. Grace	Australia	The Oval	1880
138	P.B.H. May	South Africa	Leeds	1951
126*	M.J. Prior	West Indies	Lord's	2007
119	I.J.L. Trott	Australia	The Oval	2009

In the 'Golden Age' of Cricket, from 1890 to 1914, Ranji was the brightest light, passing 3,000 runs in both 1899 and 1900 in exquisite style and ending that period with the highest batting average of anyone scoring at least 10,000 runs.

Player	Runs	Avge
K.S. Ranjitsinhji	**24,653**	**56.80**
C.B. Fry	30,235	**50.56**
W.W. Armstrong	12,949	**45.27**
V.T. Trumper	16,939	**44.57**
C. Hill	17,022	**43.64**

He captained Sussex for four seasons, where he formed a formidable partnership on and off the field with C.B. Fry, with whom he shared a lifelong friendship. It was Fry to whom he turned to help him with his seminal publication *The Jubilee Book of Cricket*, which examined the techniques of batting, bowling and fielding.

At the end of the 1904 season he returned to India, ascending to the throne at the end of 1906. From then on, he played three more seasons in England, this time as the ruler of a small state, still scoring runs but with other, more pressing matters on his mind.

Acknowledged as a great of the game in England, he was less appreciated in India. However, he left a lasting legacy in the country of his birth in that the Ranji Trophy, the national first-class competition for cricket in India, is named after him.

Allan Border   international career 1978–94

'You can see by his walk to the wicket, like a terrier out for a walk in the neighbourhood bristling with bigger dogs, that he is ready for a fight and not afraid of his ability to look after himself.' Christopher Martin-Jenkins

The man who lifted Australian cricket out of its mid-1980s doldrums and turned it into the world's best team was a colossus of the modern game.

Allan Border debuted for New South Wales in January 1977 and made his first Test appearance two years later at Melbourne against England. However, the big names in the Australian side had departed for World Series Cricket, and this new-look team were no match for the England tourists. He was unbeaten in both innings of his next match – at Sydney – scoring 60 and 45, but the Test was lost from a seemingly impregnable position.

In 1980, the stars returned, but by then Border was assured of his place in the side. Australia may have lost their series in Pakistan, but Border became the first – and so far only – Test batsman to post two scores of at least 150 in the same Test.

Player	Scores	Match	Venue	Year
A.R. Border	150* & 153	Australia v Pakistan	Lahore	1980

Ian Botham hijacked the 1981 Ashes, but Border ended the series by batting for fifteen hours between dismissals in compiling 123 not out at Old Trafford and then 106 not out and 84 at The Oval. All that was achieved in a losing effort and with a broken finger on his left hand.

Eighteen months later, he nearly brought about one of the greatest of all Test victories at Melbourne when he was joined by last man Jeff Thomson with 74 more runs needed. Slowly they closed the gap until just 4 runs were required to win. But then Thomson edged Botham to slip, where Chris Tavaré parried the ball to Geoff Miller to complete the victory for England.

After the combined retirements of Chappell, Lillee and Marsh, Kim Hughes was appointed Australian captain. However, his reign was short and ended in a tearful resignation at Brisbane in November 1984. So, more by default than by anything else, the reins were thrust in Border's direction.

It didn't start well, with home and away defeats to New Zealand, coupled with Ashes defeats in 1985 and then at home in 1986/87. Border's was the wicket that the English prized the most, but it didn't help the results. He did taste success, leading Australia to a surprise World Cup triumph in the subcontinent in 1987, memorably dismissing Mike Gatting in the final to an ill-advised reverse sweep.

After carrying the team on the shoulders of his run-making for so long, more players started to develop around him and he successfully turned a group of youngsters into a world-class team. By the time the 1989 Ashes series in England rolled around he was out for revenge with a new attitude.

It was one-way traffic as the urn was regained 4-0 and a new breed of Australian cricketer was born, with a tough, no-nonsense attitude. David Boon, Mark Taylor and the Waugh twins took responsibility for the run-scoring and Terry Alderman, Merv Hughes, Craig McDermott and Bruce Reid took the wickets. And then, in 1992, along came Shane Warne.

Border still had one more Ashes series in him, which was another triumph – his unbeaten 200 at Leeds highlighting a 4-1 Australian victory in 1993 – and he retired the following year with a then record 156 Tests, 11,174 runs and 156 catches to his name. His last 153 Test appearances had been in a row, setting a record that was to last for more than twenty years.

Matches	Player	Team	From	Until
159	A.N. Cook	Eng	May 2006	Sep 2018
153	**A.R. Border**	**Aus**	**Mar 1979**	**Mar 1994**
107	M.E. Waugh	Aus	Jun 1993	Oct 2002
106	S.M. Gavaskar	Ind	Jan 1975	Feb 1987
101	B.B. McCullum	NZ	Mar 2004	Feb 2016

A measure of the man is the fact that the leading Australian cricketer of the year is awarded the Allan Border Medal. He may not have been the most stylish batsman but he was the main reason why Australia became the dominant cricketing force in the last years of the twentieth century.

Ricky Ponting **international career 1995–2012**

'He's our greatest batsman after Bradman.' Julia Gillard

Born in Launceston, Ricky Ponting was a sporting prodigy early on, ruining a Tasmania Under-13 cricket week for everyone else by scoring four centuries. That earned him promotion to the Under-16 side, where he scored two more. His prodigious scoring in youth cricket led to a first-class debut at the age of just 17 for Tasmania, and he was not overawed, scoring 56 against South Australia.

At the age of 20, he made 96 on his Test debut – the victim of a debatable lbw decision by umpire Khizar Hayat off Chaminda Vaas at Perth. 'You'd have to say Ponting was a little bit unlucky,' was the view at the time of commentator Tony Greig. From that moment on, it was almost as if he had decided to make up for that disappointment.

There were early setbacks and well-documented clashes with authority but eighteen months later, he lit up Headingley with his first Test century – an innings of 127 – and he was here to stay. His prolific run-making only really faltered very late in his career, which precipitated his eventual retirement, but he still ended with far more runs in international cricket than any other Australian.

Player	Matches	Runs	100s
R.T. Ponting	559	27,368	70
S.R. Waugh	493	18,496	35
A.R. Border	429	17,698	30
M.J. Clarke	394	17,112	36
M.E. Waugh	372	16,529	38

He became a key member of the Australian side that usurped the West Indies to become the undisputed number one Test team in the mid-1990s. As with many of the greatest players, he eventually graduated to captaincy, leading his team to victory in both the 2003 and 2007 World Cups, scoring an undefeated 140 in the former final against India at Johannesburg.

He was fortunate to have inherited a fine team from Steve Waugh, who in turn inherited a fine one from Mark Taylor, but he was never better than when he first took over the reins, averaging 67.93 over a seventy-two-Test stretch from 2001/02 to 2008, silencing any critics of his captaincy.

Glenn McGrath and Shane Warne played twenty-four Tests together under Ponting's captaincy, and Australia won nineteen of those Tests, drawing the other five. In his other fifty-three Tests in charge, Australia were more fallible, winning twenty-nine and losing sixteen. Never was this more exemplified than in the 2005 Ashes series, when Australia won the First Test at Lord's, but lost both the lead and the series after McGrath accidentally trod on a ball during training. It could have been worse had it not been for Ponting's final-day innings of 156 at Old Trafford, which saved the match.

The 2005 series lives long in the memory, but Ponting's copybook was blotted slightly by leading Australia to two other Ashes series defeats, including one at home in 2010/11, but no one has come close to his 108 Test match victories.

Player	Team	Matches	Won	Lost	Tied	Drawn
R.T. Ponting	**Aus**	**168**	**108**	**31**	**0**	**29**
S.K. Warne	Aus	145	**92**	26	0	27
S.R. Waugh	Aus	168	**86**	36	1	45
G.D. McGrath	Aus	124	**84**	20	0	20
J.H. Kallis	SA	166	**82**	42	0	42

Whereas some criticised his captaincy, no one can deny his place in the very highest echelons of batsmen. And despite appearances to the contrary, he is quick to point out that he did possess more than just the pull shot!

Javed Miandad   international career 1975–96

'Viv Richards merely made it look as though you weren't good enough to bowl to him. Miandad said it to your face.' Gideon Haigh

For years, Javed Miandad was the *enfant terrible* of Pakistani cricket – people just loved to hate him the world over – but there was no denying the quality of his batsmanship. He was able to combine his desire for a fight with an aggressive technique, in which he could play every stroke in *The MCC Cricket Coaching Book* – and a few more besides.

Born in Karachi, Miandad was spotted by former Pakistan captain Abdul Hafeez Kardar, who called him the 'Find of the Decade', and he was soon playing first-class cricket for Karachi Whites at the tender age of 16, scoring 50 in his first innings. At 17, he became the youngest player to score a first-class triple century when he struck 311 against National Bank of Pakistan in the final of the Kardar Summer Shield.

He soon made his way into the Test team and, still in his teens, made his debut against New Zealand at Lahore. His side were soon in trouble at 55-4, but that didn't seem to faze the youngster. He added 281 for the fifth wicket with Asif Iqbal, and scored 163 before becoming the first victim in a hat-trick by fellow debutant Peter Petherick.

He followed up three weeks later with an innings of 206 at Karachi, becoming the youngest player to score a maiden Test double-century – a record that still stands.

Age	Score	Player	Match	Venue	Year
19y 140d	**206**	**Javed Miandad**	**Pakistan v New Zealand**	**Karachi**	**1976**
20y 308d	223	G.A. Headley	West Indies v England	Kingston	1930
21y 32d	224	V.G. Kambli	India v England	Bombay	1993
21y 213d	365*	G.S. Sobers	West Indies v Pakistan	Kingston	1958
21y 259d	200	G.C. Smith	South Africa v Bangladesh	East London	2002

Miandad's Test batting average never dropped below 50 and he finally retired at the end of 1993 with it sitting at 52.57. He was also prolific in ODI cricket, becoming the first player to participate in six World Cups, and his feat of scoring nine successive ODI fifties is unlikely to ever be broken.

50s	Player	Team	Start	End
9	**Javed Miandad**	**Pak**	**Mar 1987**	**Oct 1987**
6	C.G. Greenidge	WI	Dec 1979	May 1980
6	A.H. Jones	NZ	Dec 1988	Mar 1989
6	M.E. Waugh	Aus	Jan 1999	Jan 1999
6	Mohammad Yousuf	Pak	Sep 2003	Oct 2003
6	K.S. Williamson	NZ	Jun 2015	Aug 2015
6	L.R.P.L. Taylor	NZ	Mar 2018	Jan 2019

It was in this format that perhaps his defining feat occurred. Just say 'Miandad's six' to any cricket fan and they will instantly recall the final of the 1986 Austral-Asia Cup at Sharjah. Pakistan needed 4 off the last ball of the match from Chetan Sharma with Miandad on strike and just one wicket in hand. Sharma's full toss sailed out of the ground and it took India a long time to recover from the psychological upset.

He was not shy of making different headlines either; his spat with Dennis Lillee at Perth brought about one of the most famous cricket photos of all time and his clashes with Imran Khan occasionally actually brought out the best in both of them – such as the memorable 1992 World Cup triumph. After two early wickets, Imran and Javed added 139 for Pakistan's third wicket to set them on their way to their eventual winning total of 249-6.

The new generation of Pakistani batting talent benefitted from his long career and attitude, not to mention his appetite for scoring runs. Even though some of his national batting records have been surpassed, he is remembered as possibly the greatest of all Pakistani batsmen.

Graeme Pollock   **international career 1963–70**

'Two things that stood out when Pollock batted; he didn't seem to hit the ball hard and yet it always beat the chaser to the boundary, and rarely did he hit a firm shot at a fieldsman.' Ian Chappell

When Donald Bradman was asked to name the best left-handers he had ever seen, he picked out Garry Sobers and Graeme Pollock. Pollock's Test career, which was ended at the age of 26 by circumstances beyond his control, was already a great one. In his twenty-three Tests he had scored 2,256 runs at an average of 60.97, which is third among batsmen with at least 2,000 Test runs.

Player	Team	Runs	Avge
D.G. Bradman	Aus	6,996	**99.94**
S.P.D. Smith	Aus	7,227	**62.84**
R.G. Pollock	**SA**	**2,256**	60.97
G.A. Headley	WI	2,190	**60.83**
H. Sutcliffe	Eng	4,555	**60.73**

There could have been fewer more competitive back garden Tests than those played out in Durban between Graeme and his older brother Peter – who was to go on to take 116 wickets in twenty-eight Tests for South Africa. At the start, Graeme also bowled fast, and once scored a century and took all ten wickets in the same match for his school while under the careful eye of his coach, former Sussex batsman George Cox.

Both Pollock brothers attended Grey High School, where Graeme found himself in the school First XI at the age of 13. He spent four years in the team, scoring more runs than anyone before, and made his first-class debut for Eastern Province in the Currie Cup at just 16. In just his fifth match he reached three figures for the first time, at 16 years 335 days the youngest to score a century in the competition, and to this date, only Daryll Cullinan among South Africans has scored a century at a younger age.

His off-side play was elegant, full of cuts and square drives, which came naturally to him. He had to work harder to score on the leg side, but his fluency increased over time. The fact that he was a strokemaker always gave the bowler hope that they might end up having the better of him, but few did.

He scored two centuries against the Australians before turning 20, and his innings of 125 at Trent Bridge in conditions conducive to swing bowling in 1965 he considered his masterpiece. With Peter picking up ten wickets in the same match, it was the brothers who won the Test for the visitors.

The runs continued to flow, with Australia treated to the tune of 209 at Cape Town in the 1967 New Year Test. However, with the cancellation of England's 1968/69 tour due to the 'D'Oliveira Affair', he had to wait three years before tasting Test cricket again, which would prove to be South Africa's final series before their sporting isolation.

In the Second Test of that series against Australia, he hit 274 at Durban, setting a record for South Africa, and the home team went on to win the series 4-0. He turned down every approach to play county cricket in England and so had to content himself with unofficial Tests against rebel tourists from England, Sri Lanka, West Indies and Australia, distinguishing himself with five centuries in sixteen matches. He also scored the first double-hundred in List A cricket, which remains one of the highest individual scores in that form of the game to this day.

Score	Player	Match	Venue	Year
268	A.D. Brown	Surrey v Glamorgan	The Oval	2002
264	R.G. Sharma	India v Sri Lanka	Kolkata	2014
257	D.J.M. Short	Western Australia v Queensland	Sydney – H	2018
248	S. Dhawan	India A v South Africa A	Pretoria	2013
237*	M.J. Guptill	New Zealand v West Indies	Wellington – W	2015
229*	B.R. Dunk	Tasmania v Queensland	Sydney – NSO	2014
222*	**R.G. Pollock**	**Eastern Province v Border**	**East London**	**1974**
222	J.M. How	Central Districts v Northern Districts	Hamilton	2013

Peter May   international career 1951–61

'I didn't see Peter May, but even Ray Illingworth said he was tremendous. For him to say that about somebody with three initials who had a southern background and went to public school, he must have been good.' Michael Atherton

There was a time when England ruled the world. By backdating the ICC Test Championship table, for most of the second half of the 1950s England would have occupied top position. The figurehead of that side and classic batting hero to an idolising generation of schoolboys was Peter May.

He performed supreme feats of scoring for his school, Charterhouse, making 1,794 runs in his four years in the school's First XI, eventually establishing his reputation as the finest schoolboy batsman in the country. In the autumn of 1949, he started studying at Cambridge University, in the days when the undergraduates could boast as strong a batting line-up as most counties, with four Cambridge men selected to attend the Test Trial at Bradford the following year.

His batting technique was near perfect, honed on the flat pitches of Charterhouse and Fenner's. Few hit the ball straighter, but he was also adept at the sweep and late cut. It says much of him that his trademark stroke was the powerful on drive – considered one of the most difficult of all to play – the power coming from impeccable timing rather than any brute strength.

He picked up the mantle as England's leading batsman, which Wally Hammond had passed to Len Hutton, and this became evident from the moment he struck 138 on his Test debut against South Africa in 1951. Having lost the Ashes the previous winter in Australia, England were not to lose another Test series for eight years. It was no coincidence that in seven of those eight years, Surrey – featuring May, Jim Laker and Tony Lock – won the County Championship.

He took over as England captain from Len Hutton and his total of forty-one Tests in charge lasted until Mike Atherton overtook it in 1997.

Captain	Matches	Won	Lost	Drawn
A.N. Cook	59	24	22	13
M.A. Atherton	54	13	21	20
M.P. Vaughan	51	26	11	14
A.J. Strauss	50	24	11	15
N. Hussain	45	17	15	13
P.B.H. May	**41**	**20**	**10**	**11**

Having won the Ashes thanks to Laker's forty-six wickets in 1956, May reached the pinnacle of his powers against the West Indies at Edgbaston in 1957. Using his front pad to great effect, he prevented a repeat of the defeat from seven years earlier and ended unbeaten on 285, sharing a fourth-wicket partnership of 411 with Colin Cowdrey, which remains England's record for any wicket.

Wicket	Runs	Partners	Against	Venue	Year
4	**411**	**P.B.H. May & M.C. Cowdrey**	**West Indies**	**Birmingham**	**1957**
6	**399**	B.A. Stokes & J.M. Bairstow	South Africa	Cape Town	2016
2	**382**	L. Hutton & M. Leyland	Australia	The Oval	1938
3	**370**	W.J. Edrich & D.C.S. Compton	South Africa	Lord's	1947
2	**369**	J.H. Edrich & K.F. Barrington	New Zealand	Leeds	1965

Ramadhin would end up bowling ninety-eight overs in the innings, but the threat was nullified, and England went on to win the series 3-0. New Zealand were trounced 4-0 in 1958 but the following winter saw a rejuvenated Australian team win back the Ashes by a similarly heavy margin.

His second-ball dismissal to Richie Benaud in the 1961 Manchester Test lived long in his memory as it precipitated a collapse from 150 for two to 201 all out. The fact that it sealed the Ashes helped lead to his retirement at the premature age of just 32. The country hoped for a comeback, with Wisden only publishing a tribute in its 1971 edition. Nevertheless, he will always be remembered as the last of England's truly great amateur batsmen.

Virat Kohli   **international career 2008–20**

'He is just an unbelievable batsman. No need to say more.' Brian Lara

Just as India's batting hero mantle was passed from Sunil Gavaskar to Sachin Tendulkar, it was subsequently passed on again to Virat Kohli, who took the 2010s by storm to become the greatest run-scorer and century-maker in all international cricket in any decade.

Player	Team	Decade	Runs	100s
V. Kohli	Ind	2010s	20,960	69
R.T. Ponting	Aus	2000s	18,962	55
J.H. Kallis	SA	2000s	16,777	38
D.P.M.D. Jayawardene	SL	2000s	16,304	34
K.C. Sangakkara	SL	2000s	15,999	31

For all his dominance in the shorter formats of the game, Kohli is all too conscious of the need to keep Test cricket alive. Possessing a technique suited to every condition and every form of the game, he evolved into the dominating force in world cricket of the decade.

He first hit the headlines in Kuala Lumpur in 2008, when he captained India to victory in the Under-19 World Cup. He scored 235 runs in that tournament, but it wasn't just the runs he scored but his attitude that stood out. It says much for him that he has managed to transform himself from a brash youth into an international superstar. Equally adept against pace and spin, he has remarkably quick wrists and nimble feet. He picks length quickly, which enables him to be decisive in his movements.

Even as India won the 2011 World Cup, he did not set the world alight, despite scoring a century in his first match against Bangladesh, but it was the following winter's tour to Australia that first marked him out for greatness. He struck his maiden Test century at Adelaide and his unbeaten innings of 133 from just eighty-six balls against Sri Lanka in the CB Series match at Hobart made a mockery of the victory target of 321. It was the first of three successive centuries in ODI cricket and marked him out as a true master of the run-chase.

He had his first taste of Test captaincy at Adelaide in December 2014 with MS Dhoni injured. India were set 364 to win in ninety-eight overs on the final day and, typical of his attitude, they decided to go for it. They were sitting pretty at 205-2 at tea, but despite the second of Kohli's two centuries in the game, they fell short by 49 runs. Not for Kohli the defensive leadership so often associated with Indian captains, but he was the first since Tiger Pataudi to risk potential defeat in pursuit of victory.

When Dhoni eventually retired from the longer form, Kohli took over as the captain on a full-time basis and his run-scoring reached even greater heights. He made three double-centuries in 2016 and three more the following year, upping his career-best score a record fifteen times.

Having struggled against the swinging ball to average just 14 on his first Test tour of England in 2014, he was determined to put things right when the opportunity next arose. He did that and plenty more in 2018, scoring 593 runs in the five-match series despite his side losing 4-1. He consoled himself a few months later by becoming the fastest batsman to score 10,000 ODI runs, in more than fifty fewer innings than the next-fastest.

Player	Team	Innings
V. Kohli	**Ind**	**205**
S.R. Tendulkar	Ind	**259**
S.C. Ganguly	Ind	**263**
R.T. Ponting	Aus	**266**
J.H. Kallis	SA	**272**
MS Dhoni	Ind	**274**
B.C. Lara	WI	**278**

His thirst for runs continued unabated in every form of the game and, at the time of writing, even Tendulkar's record of 100 international centuries does not seem too much of a pipe dream.

Neil Harvey   international career 1948–63

'Neil Harvey always had sunlight gleaming across his cricket.' David Frith

Neil Harvey's scores in his first nine Tests were so extraordinary that they warrant printing in full: 13, 153, 112, 4*, 17, 34, 178, 23*, 2, 151*, 56*, 100 and 116, giving 959 runs at an average of 106.55, with six hundreds – all achieved before turning 22 years old.

He was fortunate in that he had five brothers, and as soon as he was old enough to hold a bat, he joined in the family matches. These took place in a narrow, cobbled lane close to his home, which encouraged them all to play straight. He scored his first century for North Fitzroy Central School before joining his brothers at Fitzroy Cricket Club, starting in the depths of the Fifth XI. It wasn't long before he had moved up to the first team, and he gave up his wicketkeeping to concentrate on his batting. It proved to be a good decision.

An innings of 69 for Victoria against the MCC tourists of 1946/47 when still just 18 pushed him into the minds of the selectors and he continued to score heavily at state level. He was given a debut against India the following season, when he scored 153 in his second Test, making him the youngest Australian to score a maiden Test century, a record he still holds.

Age	Score	Player	Against	Venue	Year
19y 121d	**153**	**R.N. Harvey**	**India**	**Melbourne**	**1948**
19y 149d	164	A. Jackson	England	Adelaide	1929
19y 354d	155	K.D. Walters	England	Brisbane	1965
20y 96d	115	P.J. Hughes	South Africa	Durban	2009
20y 124d	112	D.G. Bradman	England	Melbourne	1929

An automatic choice for the 1948 Ashes tour, Harvey was named twelfth man for the first three Tests thanks to his fielding prowess and finally made his way into the side for the Leeds Test, where he scored 112 and helped Australia to a memorable victory.

His first full series was against South Africa in 1949/50, and he scored 660 runs, including four centuries. Three years later, the same opposition were treated to 834 runs, which surpassed Bradman's Australian record of 806 runs in a series against South Africa. Four centuries flowed from his bat, including innings of 190 at Sydney and 205 at Melbourne. The tour of the West Indies in 1955/56 was almost as good. Australia won the series 3-0, with Harvey contributing a brace of 133s at Jamaica and Trinidad and rounding off the series with 204 when the tour returned to Jamaica. He ended up scoring more Test runs in the 1950s than anyone else.

Player	Team	Runs	100s
R.N. Harvey	**Aus**	**4,719**	**16**
P.B.H. May	Eng	**4,182**	12
E.D. Weekes	WI	**3,383**	10
L. Hutton	Eng	**3,183**	8
C.L. Walcott	WI	**3,129**	13

The only criticism his batting drew over the course of his career was that he might have been too attacking, and he perfected his fielding by playing baseball in the off season for Fitzroy. Playing as an infielder, the accuracy of his throwing enabled him to run out several unsuspecting batsmen from his favoured position of cover.

At the time of his retirement, he had 6,149 runs and twenty-one centuries – second only to Bradman among Australians at that time. His time as a selector in the 1970s coincided with two significant decisions: the removal of Bill Lawry as captain early in the decade and the appointment of 41-year-old Bobby Simpson as captain in 1977, nine years after his last Test.

Everton Weekes   international career 1948–58

'Everton Weekes was every inch a princely batsman. He was to cricket what Paul McCartney's melodies are for music.' Rajgopal Nidamboor

Another of the hallowed 'Three Ws' trio, cricket was in Everton Weekes' blood as his cousin Kenneth played two Tests on the 1939 tour of England, scoring 137 at The Oval. Having played for St Leonard's School at the age of 12, Weekes subsequently served with the Caribbean Regiment during the Second World War and caught the eye of Teddy Hoad, the former Test batsman.

Having made his first-class debut at the age of 18, he was then picked for a Test debut in early 1948. He was troubled by England's bowlers at the start of his career, and he had a highest score of just 36 in his first five innings, but an injury to George Headley meant that Weekes was included in the team for the final Test of the series at Kingston. He made the most of that opportunity, scoring 141 to help the West Indies win the Test and the series 2-0.

Seven months later, he found himself in Delhi, where the Indian attack was treated to an innings of 128 followed by 194 the following month at Mumbai. He ended 1948 with a Test at Kolkata, and not content with striking 162 in the first innings in just three hours, he doubled up with 101 second time around, making a record-breaking five successive Test hundreds, a record that stands to this day.

100s	Player	Team	Start	End
5	**E.D. Weekes**	**West Indies**	**Mar 1948**	**Dec 1948**
4	J.H.W. Fingleton	Australia	Jan 1936	Dec 1936
4	A. Melville	South Africa	Mar 1939	Jun 1947
4	R.S. Dravid	India	Aug 2002	Oct 2002

The action shifted to Chennai and he was looking good for a sixth century on the trot when a debatable run-out decision ended his quest with his score on 90.

That purple patch couldn't last forever, and he found things tougher going on the 1951/52 tour of Australia, when Lindwall and Miller resorted to trying to bounce him out. However, his form returned in spectacular fashion when he faced India again in 1953, starting the series with an innings of 207 at Port of Spain, followed by 161 in the third Test and 109 in the final match at Kingston. Another double-century was to follow against England at Port of Spain, an innings in which Worrell and Walcott also scored centuries.

New Zealand were his next victims as he returned to his habit of scoring successive centuries, reeling off three on the trot, but he was disappointing on the 1957 tour of England. His final Test hundred was an innings of 197 at Bridgetown in January 1958, but it was overshadowed by Hanif Mohammad's sixteen-hour innings of 337 in the same match.

When Weekes retired at the end of that series, he was the leading West Indian run-scorer in Test cricket, with the other two Ws in second and third place.

Player	Matches	Runs	Avge
E.D. Weekes	**48**	**4,455**	**58.61**
C.L. Walcott	42	**3,714**	58.03
F.M.M. Worrell	32	**2,691**	51.75
G.A. Headley	22	**2,190**	60.83
J.B. Stollmeyer	32	**2,159**	42.33

After retirement, he represented Barbados at bridge in major international tournaments, and was knighted for services to cricket in 1995.

Zaheer Abbas   **international career 1969–85**

'A cricket genius, Zaheer Abbas would have found a batting place in most people's imaginary "World XI" for most of his career.' Christopher Martin-Jenkins

When Zaheer Abbas first arrived in England as a spectacled 23-year-old with one Test behind him, there was nothing to mark him as anything special. By the time he retired he was renowned as one of the most elegant strokemakers of all time and the first – and so far, only – batsman from the subcontinent to score a hundred first-class centuries. To this day, only two players from outside England boast more three-figure scores.

Player	Matches	100s
D.G. Bradman	234	117
I.V.A. Richards	507	114
Zaheer Abbas	**459**	108
G.M. Turner	455	103
C.G. Greenidge	523	92

Born in Sialkot, he moved to Karachi at the age of 7 and started playing in the street with the rest of his family. Quite some family it was: four of his brothers became cricketers and the other two chose hockey. Zaheer attended Islamia College, where he scored fifty centuries, before moving to Karachi University and landing a job in the Sales Department of Pakistan International Airways.

It wasn't long before his appetite for scoring runs became clear as he extended his maiden first-class century to a score of 197 in the domestic Quaid-e-Azam Trophy. Eventually he was noticed and made his Test debut in late 1969 against New Zealand, but he failed to fire, scoring just 12 and 27, and he was discarded until the 1971 tour of England.

The First Test on that tour was at Edgbaston and he marked it with an innings of 274, which instantly attracted county suitors. He plumped for Gloucestershire and ended up scoring forty-nine centuries for his adopted team. The baton of leading batsman in the team had been passed from Wally Hammond to Tom Graveney, and in Zaheer, a suitable successor was found.

Eight times he scored two centuries in a match, and on four of those occasions one of the knocks was a double-century – an achievement no one else has managed more than twice.

Player	200 + 100
Zaheer Abbas	4
G.A. Gooch	2
M.W. Goodwin	2
M.R. Hallam	2
C.J.L. Rogers	2
N.R. Taylor	2

Despite that massive score early on, his Test career sputtered, and he did not reach three figures for another three years. When he did though, he made it count, with 240 at The Oval in 1974, and in the long, hot summer of 1976, he hit 2,554 first-class runs, with eleven centuries, all made with his characteristic grace and beautiful timing.

His international career continued with staggering peaks yet puzzling troughs, but he finally came good at home against India in 1977/78 in the first Test series between the teams for more than seventeen years. He started the series by striking 176 and 96 at Faisalabad, before hitting an unbeaten 235 in the next Test at Lahore.

He reached the peak of his powers in the early 1980s, the undoubted highlight being his innings of 215 against India at Lahore, which was his hundredth first-class century and made him just the second player to achieve the landmark in a Test match. He followed up with 186 at Karachi and 168 at Faisalabad to help Pakistan win the series 3-0.

His ODI record was superb, averaging 47.62 at a strike rate of 84.80, and he was the first player to score three successive centuries in that form of the game. To put that into context, the overall strike rate in ODI cricket over the course of his career was just 70.60 – a far cry from the exaggerated scoring rates of modern times – so he was scoring 20 per cent faster than the average batsman over that period.

C.B. Fry   international career 1896–1912

'He was one of the last of his kind – and certainly the finest specimen of it – the amateurs, the smiling gentlemen of games, intensely devoted to the skill and the struggle but always with a certain gaiety, romantic at heart but classical in style.'
J.B. Priestley

When C.B. Fry appeared on just the fifth-ever episode of *This is Your Life* in 1955, he was introduced as 'a brilliant classical scholar; he devoted forty-two years of his life to the Training Ship *Mercury*; had a distinguished career as an author and journalist; and did devoted work in the cause of world peace at Geneva'. His sporting record didn't even warrant a mention!

Episode	Subject	Claim to fame	Broadcast
1	Eamonn Andrews	Irish broadcaster	29/07/1955
2	Yvonne Bailey	Special Operations Executive agent	25/09/1955
3	Ted Ray	Comedian	23/10/1955
4	James Butterworth	Methodist minister who founded Clubland	20/11/1955
5	**C.B. Fry**	**All-round sportsman**	**18/12/1955**

After an outstanding academic and sporting school career at Repton, in which he captained both the football and cricket teams, C.B. Fry was accepted to study at Wadham College, Oxford. He excelled there, earning blues in football, cricket and athletics, not to mention equalling the world long jump record when he leapt 7.18 metres in 1893.

He toured South Africa in 1895/96, but that was to be his only tour for England as he was frequently too busy to travel abroad. Playing as a defender, he forged a football career with Southampton, and played in the 1902 FA Cup Final at Crystal Palace, losing to Sheffield United 2-1 after the initial match had ended in a 1-1 draw.

He became a permanent fixture in the England team in 1899, when W.G. Grace insisted he played in the First Ashes Test at Trent Bridge. He scored 50 in a low-scoring game and played in all five Tests of the series. Six times from 1899 to 1905 he passed 2,000 runs in a season, peaking with 3,147 in 1901, a year in which he became the first batsman to score six successive first-class centuries, which remains the world record.

100s	Player	Year(s)
6	**C.B. Fry**	**1901**
6	D.G. Bradman	1938–1939
6	M.J. Procter	1970–1971
5	E.D. Weekes	1956
5	B.C. Lara	1994
5	M.E.K. Hussey	2003
5	P.A. Patel	2007
5	K.C. Sangakkara	2017

In contrast to the mountains of runs he and his best friend Ranji scored for Sussex, Fry's international career was not an unqualified success. He struggled in the 1902 Ashes series but come 1905, he scored his maiden Test century – an innings of 144 at The Oval. That form continued when South Africa visited two years later, and he made 129 in the final Test. However, his Test average of 32.18 from his twenty-six matches was in stark contrast to his overall first-class average of 50.22, which included ninety-four centuries.

After a successful 1911 season for his new county, Hampshire, Fry was chosen to lead England in the experimental Triangular Test Tournament the following year, which also featured Australia and South Africa. Blighted from the start by unseasonably wet weather, he still managed to captain the side to four wins out of six matches to win the competition.

After retirement he was called into action as his old batting partner Ranji's deputy to the League of Nations and it was then that he supposedly wrote a famous speech outlining that the League could discuss Mussolini's occupation of Corfu. Three times he stood for Parliament but was unsuccessful each time, and there is the apocryphal story of his being offered the kingdom of Albania!

Whereas he shone brightest of all on the cricket field, his grave sums him up best: 'Cricketer, scholar, athlete, Author – The Ultimate All-rounder'.

Greg Chappell   **international career 1970–84**

'His runs were made with an aesthetic imperious quality which few others in history could emulate.' Don Bradman

If ever there was a passing of the baton, then this was it. Little did Don Bradman know that when he was dismissed for his famous duck on 14 August 1948, just seven days earlier in Adelaide, a baby had been born who would one day take his Australian run-scoring record. Bradman himself was delighted when the record went, as he appreciated the aesthetic quality that Greg Chappell brought to the crease.

You could say it was in his blood. Grandfather Vic Richardson was not only a former teammate of Bradman's but also represented his country at baseball as well as excelling in tennis, lacrosse, Australian football and golf. Older brother Ian was a willing garden adversary and also went on to captain Australia, and when Ian was off playing serious cricket, younger brother Trevor took his place.

Greg joined Glenelg Cricket Club at the age of 12, where he was coached by Lyn Fuller, who helped to refine his sublimely orthodox technique with a magisterial on drive, considered by some to be the greatest stroke in the game.

He was a relative veteran of the first-class scene when he made his Test debut at Perth in 1970, having enjoyed two productive seasons with Somerset as an overseas player. He marked the occasion with a century as well as dismissing Colin Cowdrey to take a First Test wicket. If that First Test innings secured his place in the team, his 131 at Lord's in 'Massie's Match' in 1972 cemented his position as one of the greats.

In March 1974, he scored 247 not out and 133 against New Zealand at Wellington, a match in which brother Ian scored 145 and 121. His total of 380 runs in the match stood as a world record for sixteen years, and to this day, only one Australian has surpassed it.

Player	Runs	Against	Venue	Year
M.A. Taylor	426	Pakistan	Peshawar	1998
G.S. Chappell	**380**	**New Zealand**	**Wellington**	**1974**
M.L. Hayden	380	Zimbabwe	Perth	2003
K.D. Walters	345	West Indies	Sydney	1969
D.A. Warner	335	Pakistan	Adelaide	2019

When England visited in 1974/75, Lillee and Thomson stole most of the headlines, but Chappell played as big a part, scoring 608 runs in the series, and equalling the world record at the time with seven catches in the Test at Perth. He went on to succeed his brother as captain and promptly led the team to a 5-1 victory over the might of the West Indies – Roberts, Holding, Gibbs and all – making 702 runs in the process.

He was possibly at his best during the years of World Series Cricket, in which he totalled 1,415 runs in just fourteen 'Tests' with an unbeaten innings of 246 against the World XI, which he considered to be his best.

For all his batting triumphs, his copybook was somewhat blotted by the infamous 'underarm' incident featuring his brother Trevor against New Zealand, which even prompted criticism from both Australian and New Zealand prime ministers.

He signed off from Test cricket with an innings of 182 against Pakistan at Sydney in January 1984, in which he not only surpassed Bradman's run aggregate record for Australia, but also became the first player to score a century in his first and last Test innings.

Player	Team	Innings	Years
G.S. Chappell	**Aus**	**108 & 182**	**1970–1984**
M. Azharuddin	Ind	110 & 102	1984–2000

That match also saw the end of the Test careers of Dennis Lillee and Rodney Marsh – together with the end of an era in Australian cricket.

Clive Lloyd   international career 1966–85

'Clive Lloyd is like a father, big brother, guardian and guide to West Indian cricketers. We respect him because he respects himself and all of us. If Worrell led by inspiration and Sobers by example, Lloyd combines both to great effect.' Joel Garner

Clive Lloyd was one of the most destructive batsmen of all time, but he will best be remembered as the mastermind behind the West Indian domination of the late 1970s and 1980s. His thick glasses seemed somewhat at odds with the heavy bat he wielded and the strength with which he struck the ball. An indication of his power is that he once held the record for the fastest double-century in first-class cricket, an innings that still ranks in the top five.

Balls	Player	Match	Venue	Year
89	Shafiqullah Shinwari	Kabul Region v Boost Region	Asadabad	2018
123	R.J. Shastri	Bombay v Baroda	Bombay	1985
123	A.H.T. Donald	Glamorgan v Derbyshire	Colwyn Bay	2016
124	**C.H. Lloyd**	**West Indians v Glamorgan**	**Swansea**	**1976**
128	D.R. Martyn	Yorkshire v Gloucestershire	Leeds	2003

Lloyd developed young and was already representing Demerara School at the age of 10. He could bat, bowl a variety of different paces and spin the ball prodigiously, while setting new standards in the field. His long strides enabled him to cover ground quickly, and he had a powerful throw and safe pair of hands.

Having made his first-class debut in 1964, his fielding prowess enabled him to make an appearance as a substitute when Australia visited Guyana for a Test match the following year. His maiden first-class century soon followed with an innings of 107 against Barbados – made after he had been dismissed by Garry Sobers for a duck in his first innings.

His Test career started with a bang, with twin innings of 82 and 78 not out against India at Mumbai in 1966, and a maiden century arrived just over a year later against England at Trinidad, swiftly followed by an innings of 129 in his first Test in Australia.

On Wes Hall's recommendation, he decided to spend some time playing league cricket in England, and he was soon signed up by Haslingden, which started a love affair with the county of Lancashire that endures to this day. He was the leading run-scorer in both his summers in the Lancashire League, with 861 runs in 1967 and 1,136 the following year.

Having been outbid by Nottinghamshire for Garry Sobers' services, Lancashire turned their attention to Lloyd, who quickly agreed to join them for the 1969 season once the West Indian tour was over. With Lloyd in their ranks, Lancashire dominated the domestic one-day scene in the 1970s, lifting five trophies.

As well as he was performing for Lancashire, his international form started to suffer, and he went a period of seventeen Tests without a century before returning to form with an innings of 178 against Australia on his home ground at Georgetown in 1973. After that, he never looked back and by the time the team travelled to India in 1974/75, he had become the captain. The following summer he scored a century in the final as his side became the inaugural World Cup winners.

The following summer was the game changer. Humiliated 5-1 in Australia by Dennis Lillee and Jeff Thomson, India then chased down a target of 403 at Port of Spain when Lloyd's spinners let him down. Never again would that be the case and the team enjoyed continuous success.

Tony Greig's England side didn't know what had hit them in the long, hot summer of 1976, and the West Indies retained their World Cup trophy in 1979 with superlative pace bowling and exciting batting. His leadership culminated in the first-ever 'blackwash' over England in 1984, when the Test series was won 5-0.

He led in eighteen Test series, winning fourteen, drawing two and only losing two. To this day, no one has had the honour of captaining the West Indies on more occasions in Test cricket.

Player	Matches
C.H. Lloyd	**74**
I.V.A. Richards	**50**
B.C. Lara	**47**
G.S. Sobers	**39**
J.O. Holder	**32**

Ken Barrington   **international career 1955–68**

'Whenever I see Ken coming to the wicket, I imagine the Union Jack fluttering behind him.' Wally Grout

Perhaps Wally Grout's quote is unsurprising, as Ken Barrington grew up with a father who spent nearly thirty years in the military and had fought in both world wars. It was he who introduced his son to cricket, but young Ken left school at the age of 14 to work in a garage.

In his teenage years he considered himself primarily a leg-spinner but opportunity knocked for him at the age of 16 when he was twirling his leggies for Reading Wednesday, who were playing at Guildford. An impressed spectator tipped off Surrey, who found a spot for him in their Colts team, for whom he played the rest of the season.

He joined the army and spent two years in Germany before returning to Surrey, where he was taken under the watchful eye of Andy Sandham – scorer of 107 first-class centuries. Sandham helped develop him into a stylish batsman as there seemed little chance of him breaking into a team already boasting Jim Laker and Tony Lock as spinners.

After a modest start in 1953, he struck three centuries the following year and international honours came in 1955, when he played two Tests against South Africa. Unfortunately, he started with a duck at Trent Bridge, and he was discarded after the next match at Lord's, only to return to the England team four years later.

It was the sunny summer of 1959 that changed everything for Barrington. In all matches, he scored 2,499 runs with six centuries, and earned a recall to play India. He subsequently made three scores in the 80s and from then on, he was pretty much an automatic selection.

It wasn't just the volume of runs that he scored, but also the fact that he played hard and with fun. Not only was he a great batsman, but he was arguably an even greater man, and he became one of the most popular players to ever don an England sweater. What also helped his cause was that he ended his career with the highest batting average by any post-war England player who scored at least a thousand runs.

Player	Matches	Runs	Avge
K.F. Barrington	**82**	**6,806**	**58.67**
L. Hutton	66	5,626	**54.62**
D.C.S. Compton	70	5,339	**49.89**
J.E. Root	97	7,823	**47.99**
E.R. Dexter	62	4,502	**47.89**

Barrington hit centuries in four successive Tests in the subcontinent in 1961/62, and then added 594 runs the following winter in the Ashes series against Richie Benaud's powerful Australian side. His highest Test score of 256 came in the batathon, which was the 1964 Old Trafford Test in which Bobby Simpson made 311. It remains the highest post-war individual score for England in Ashes cricket.

Score	Player	Venue	Year
256	**K.F. Barrington**	**Manchester**	**1964**
244*	A.N. Cook	Melbourne	2017
235*	A.N. Cook	Brisbane	2010
227	K.P. Pietersen	Adelaide	2010
215	D.I. Gower	Birmingham	1985

After being diagnosed with thrombosis, he announced his retirement but continued to serve English cricket. He was part of the selection committee who appointed Tony Greig England captain and recalled Brian Close and John Edrich to face the might of the 1976 West Indies machine. He subsequently managed several English touring sides and oversaw the controversial Ian Botham-led 1981 tour of the Caribbean, when he suffered a fatal heart attack – in the same city of Bridgetown in which he had scored his maiden Test century back in 1960.

AB de Villiers   international career 2004–18

'AB is like a mind-reading bloodhound. He can smell the emotions of the opposition and he predicts what they are going to do and how they will behave.' Dale Steyn

Every so often, among the mundane nicknames that nowadays seem to proliferate in top-class sport, there emerges a great one that sums a player up, while remaining catchy. 'Mr 360' was perfect. It combined de Villiers' ability to strike any delivery to any part of the field and reminded everyone that he wasn't just a one-trick pony. He was able to reach the top in all three forms of the game, blending innovation with classic strokeplay.

The cricket public never saw the hours of practice that went into everything he did. To them he appeared to be the guy who could do it all. He had an opportunity to travel to Nick Bollettieri's tennis academy in Florida when he was 13 years old, but his parents were not keen for him to go at the time. He was also a talented golfer and received an offer to sign for a provincial rugby side at the age of 18. He turned that down too in order to concentrate on his cricket.

He first caught the eye in the summer of 2003, when he scored 143 for South Africa Under-19s against their English counterparts at Arundel. Also on that tour were his school friend Faf du Plessis and other future Protea teammates J.P. Duminy and Vernon Philander.

Soon after returning home to South Africa, he made his first-class debut for Northerns in the SuperSport Series, scoring a pair of half-centuries, and it came as no surprise to anyone when he was fast-tracked into the Test team the following season.

Debuting in the same Test as Dale Steyn, they were destined to become the most famous pair of simultaneous debutants since Sachin Tendulkar and Waqar Younis began their Test careers opposing each other at Karachi in November 1989. De Villiers made 28 and 14 while Steyn conceded nearly 5 an over as England cantered to a seven-wicket triumph with no hint of the greatness to follow for either of them.

The epitome of the modern cricketer, de Villiers proved himself to be not just a jack of all trades, but a master of all trades over the course of his international career. Unlike others whose batting form declined when they took the gloves in Test cricket, he averaged 57.41 in his twenty-four Tests when given the gloves – the highest batting average for anyone keeping wicket in at least twenty Tests.

Player	Team	Matches	Runs	Avge
AB de Villiers	**SA**	**24**	**2,067**	**57.41**
A. Flower	Zim	55	4,404	**53.70**
A.C. Gilchrist	Aus	96	5,570	**47.60**
L.E.G. Ames	Eng	44	2,387	**43.40**
B.J. Watling	NZ	60	3,252	**41.16**

He also has two Test wickets and a pop album release under his belt.

De Villiers set a new South African Test record individual score of 278 not out in 2010 and then turned his attention to record-setting in the shorter form of the game. He struck both the fastest 50 (in sixteen balls) and century (thirty-one balls) against the West Indies in January 2015, and then subjected the same opposition to the fastest 150, which not only came in the World Cup that year, but bettered Shane Watson's previous mark at the time by nineteen deliveries.

Balls	Player	Match	Venue	Year
64	**AB de Villiers**	**South Africa v West Indies**	**Sydney**	**2015**
76	J.C. Buttler	England v West Indies	St George's	2019
83	S.R. Watson	Australia v Bangladesh	Mirpur	2011
85	Sharjeel Khan	Pakistan v Ireland	Dublin – M	2016
85	C.H. Gayle	West Indies v England	St George's	2019

As with many of the leading players in international teams, captaincy eventually came knocking as Hashim Amla resigned the Test helm in early 2016. However, de Villiers was only to captain the national side in three Tests, laid low with an elbow injury before resigning the post at the end of the year. He made a brief return to the longer form, before retiring from all international cricket in 2018, at the age of just 34.

Steve Waugh   **international career 1985–2004**

'Like some immutable law of physics, Steve Waugh has always saved his best for the most unpromising situations.' Derek Pringle

Born four minutes before his twin brother Mark, the scene was immediately set for years of games of back garden cricket featuring their contrasting abilities – Mark the more stylish but Steve the more determined and competitive. They were both selected to play for their local Bankstown district side at the age of 8, while also helping their school win a statewide soccer competition. Football and cricket ran in parallel until the age of 17, when cricket's greater time demands took priority.

In early 1985, Steve won an Esso scholarship to England to play for Essex and while there made headlines by striking a twenty-eight-ball century for Ilford against Chingford on a wet wicket in the Bertie Joel Cup. Chingford exacted some measure of revenge in the return fixture a few weeks later, when he was dismissed for just 5.

The retirements of the triumvirate of Chappell, Lillee and Marsh in 1984, combined with a 'rebel' team visiting South Africa, meant that suddenly, opportunities opened up in the Australian Test team, and after just eleven first-class matches, Steve found himself facing India at the MCG in the 1985 Boxing Day Test.

He had to immediately learn on the job, and it was as much his medium-pace bowling as his batting that kept him in the team as he only passed 50 once in his first nine Tests. However, in 1988 a back injury to Martin Crowe meant that Somerset were suddenly in need of a new overseas player, and it was to Steve Waugh – who was playing in the Birmingham League for Smethwick – that they turned in their hour of need.

He was a revelation, passing 1,000 runs in only eleven innings, and ending the season with six hundreds.

Nevertheless, despite that recent success in England, he came into the 1989 Ashes series with a batting average of 30.52 in his twenty-six Tests without a century. He had taken forty wickets at 39.32 and had helped Australia win the 1987 World Cup, but those figures were hardly those of a world-beating all-rounder. But come that summer, everything changed.

England just couldn't get him out as he struck 177 and 152 – both unbeaten in the first two Tests – and suddenly, his batting average was 40. That wasn't an

Jack Hobbs (L) and Herbert Sutcliffe (R) walk out to bat for England against Australia at Trent Bridge in 1926.

Chris Gayle, the most prolific Twenty20 batsman of all time, and not a bad Test player either.

Alastair Cook, England's leading Test run-scorer.

Viv Richards, the uncrowned king of Caribbean batsme

Donald Bradman, whose Test batting average of 99.94 appears to be a misprint.

Brian Lara, whose insatiable appetite for run-scoring gave him the highest individual scores in Test and first-class cricket.

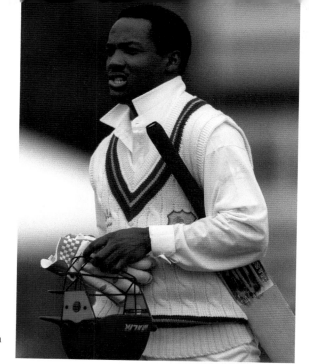

Virat Kohli scored more international runs in the 2010s than any other batsman in any decade in history.

W.G. Grace, who found cricket a country pastime and left it a national institution.

Jacques Kallis, who won more 'Player of the Match' awards than any other Test cricketer.

MS Dhoni earned more money from the IPL than any other player.

Adam Gilchrist changed the role of the wicketkeeper for good.

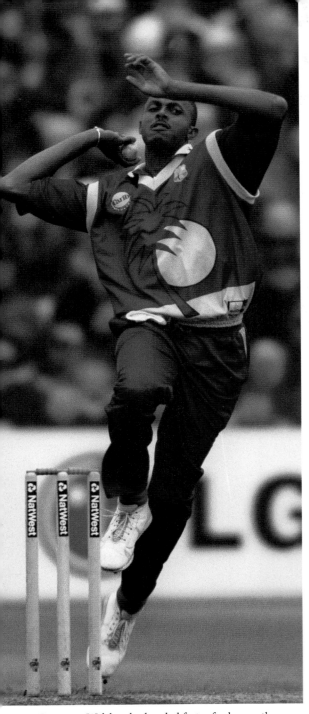

Courtney Walsh, who bowled faster for longer than anyone else.

Wasim Akram, the only left-arm fast bowler to take at least 400 Test wickets.

Glenn McGrath went from living in a caravan to taking more Test wickets than any other seamer at the time of his retirement in 2007.

Muttiah Muralitharan, the leading wicket-taker (1,347) in all international cricket.

Shane Warne, who revolutionised leg-spin bowling in the 1990s.

immediate springboard to greatness as his form subsequently fell away, and over the course of eleven Tests over 1990, 1991 and 1992, he averaged just 17.31, and at one stage was dropped in favour of his twin brother Mark. But there was nothing like a 1990s Ashes series to get those averages soaring! Steve didn't disappoint, with 416 runs in 1993, and for the rest of his career he averaged 58 and retired having played more Tests than anyone else.

It was his double-hundred in Jamaica in 1995 that signified the changing of the guard from the West Indies to Australia as the dominant Test team, and it was a position they were not to relinquish for a decade. Steve also enjoyed continued success against England – scoring memorable twin centuries on a tricky pitch in the 1997 Old Trafford Test and reaching a fairy-tale century from the last ball of the day on his home ground of the SCG in 2003.

He also captained Australia to victory in the 1999 World Cup – the first of three successive triumphs – which featured the nerve-shredding semi-final at Edgbaston against South Africa. Later that year they set a record for the most successive Test match victories.

Matches	Team	Start	Finish
16	**Australia**	**Oct 1999**	**Feb 2001**
16	Australia	Dec 2005	Jan 2008
11	West Indies	Mar 1984	Dec 1984
9	Sri Lanka	Aug 2001	Mar 2002
9	South Africa	Mar 2002	May 2003

Steve Waugh had his detractors who pointed at his arguably selfish batting, but no one who has captained his team on at least twenty occasions has enjoyed a better Test record.

Captain	Team	Matches	Won	Lost	Drawn	% Won
S.R. Waugh	Aus	57	41	9	7	71.92
D.G. Bradman	Aus	24	15	3	6	62.50
R.T. Ponting	Aus	77	48	16	13	62.33
V. Kohli	Ind	55	33	12	10	60.00
A.L. Hassett	Aus	24	14	4	6	58.33

Rahul Dravid   international career 1996–2012

'Try to take his wicket in the first 15 minutes. If you can't then only try to take the remaining wickets.' Steve Waugh

Poor Rahul Dravid. For pretty much all his career he was overshadowed by the more famous, showier batsmen around him. Sachin Tendulkar, Sourav Ganguly and V.V.S. Laxman appeared to have greater natural ability, but over the course of his 164 Tests, he ended up facing more deliveries than any other batsman in history.

Player	Team	Balls
R. Dravid	**Ind**	**31,258**
S.R. Tendulkar	Ind	**29,437**
J.H. Kallis	SA	**28,903**
S. Chanderpaul	WI	**27,395**
A.R. Border	Aus	**27,002**

Dravid first played cricket at St Joseph's School, Bangalore, where he doubled up as their wicketkeeper. He represented Karnataka at Under-15 level, striking a double-century against Kerala, and a Ranji Trophy debut followed just after he had turned 18. He was not overawed, hitting 82 in his first innings, and he continued to score heavily at domestic level for the next few years, combining his cricket with a degree in commerce from Bangalore University. Finally, the selectors were convinced after his innings of 114 in the 1995/96 Ranji Trophy final and gave him an ODI debut.

India had already lost Navjot Singh Sidhu and Sanjay Manjrekar on the 1996 tour of England and so there were suddenly vacancies in the batting line-up for the Lord's Test. In at number three strode Sourav Ganguly – who struck 131 – and at number seven was Dravid, who worked his way serenely to 95 before edging Chris Lewis to Jack Russell. Undaunted, he then proceeded to score Test centuries in fifteen successive years from 1997 to 2011.

In his early career he suffered in comparison to the fluent Tendulkar, but it was on the 1999 tour of New Zealand that he started to emerge from the shadows. He struck twin centuries in the Hamilton Test and a run-a-ball, unbeaten 123 in the ODI at Taupo. In the 1999 World Cup he shared a partnership of 318 with Ganguly against Sri Lanka, and that November he went even better, adding 331 with Tendulkar against New Zealand at Hyderabad.

When VVS Laxman's 281 orchestrated the 'Miracle at Kolkata' in 2001, Dravid weighed in with 180 runs of his own, and the pair batted throughout the fourth day on the way to adding 376 for the fifth wicket and producing an incredible victory after India were forced to follow on. His prolific form continued on the 2002 tour of England, where he struck successive innings of 115, 148 and, finally, 217 at The Oval.

Further success came his way in Australia the following year where his double-century at Adelaide brought about another sensational triumph, and then he made his highest career score of 270 against Pakistan at Rawalpindi. With Ganguly publicly falling out with coach Greg Chappell, Dravid took over as captain and memorably led India to a series victory in England in 2007, which almost made up for the disaster in the 2007 World Cup, in which India failed to make it through the initial group stage.

He continued to produce at the highest level almost to the end of his career, batting superbly on the 2011 tour of England to score 461 runs with three centuries when the rest of the Indian batting was crumbling all around him. He also ended his career with more catches than any other fielder in Test history.

Player	Team	Matches	Catches
R. Dravid	**Ind**	**164**	**210**
D.P.M.D. Jayawardene	SL	149	**205**
J.H. Kallis	SA	166	**200**
R.T. Ponting	Aus	168	**196**
M.E. Waugh	Aus	128	**181**

Ironically, his nickname 'The Wall' came from an advertising campaign for Reebok in the early 2000s, but despite that reputation, he still scored more than 10,000 ODI runs at a respectable strike rate of 71.24.

Aravinda de Silva   international career 1984–2003

'Ari was an inspiration to me and the whole side felt the same. When he packed his bags, he hugged each of us and I have never known a professional sports team so close to tears.' Graham Cowdrey

Before the twin pillars of Sri Lankan batting of Sangakkara and Jayawardene came Aravinda de Silva, the first superstar of Sri Lankan cricket, and the man who proved that batsmen from the subcontinent could play the short ball.

He first made news with his prodigious feats of scoring for his school, D.S. Senanayake College. Standing only 5 feet 3 inches, he had to learn to play off the back foot and developed fierce cut and pull strokes early on in his career. Fortunately, he had quick feet, which enabled him to play both pace and spin with confidence and aplomb.

He made his Test debut at Lord's in 1984, in a match remembered for Sidath Wettimuny's epic innings of 190 and captain Duleep Mendis falling just short of scoring two centuries in the match. De Silva's contribution was nothing special – scoring just 16 and 3 – but his side outplayed England in their first Test in the country and won over a new legion of fans.

The following year he scored 75 as Sri Lanka recorded the first Test win in their history – defeating India at Colombo – and a first Test century followed against a Pakistan attack of Imran Khan, Wasim Akram and Abdul Qadir at Faisalabad the following month.

De Silva proved himself to be equally adept at both Test and ODI cricket, but despite his obvious talent, he was still prone to inconsistency and was frequently frustrated by getting out to careless strokes. It made matters worse in that he was a batting maestro playing for what was the weakest team in international cricket at the time. However, over time he learned to convert an attractive cameo into a beautifully crafted innings.

At Brisbane in late 1989, he faced a rampant Australian side who had just completed a comprehensive series victory against England. De Silva countered the threat of Hughes, Alderman and Lawson by scoring 167, and just over a year later he struck a then national record individual score of 267 against New Zealand at Wellington.

In 1995 he signed for Kent and was a revelation. Despite the county finishing bottom of the County Championship, he scored 1,781 runs in first-class cricket, and lit up Lord's with a scintillating innings of 112 from just ninety-five balls against Lancashire in the Benson & Hedges Cup Final. Like so many of his fine innings that summer though, it counted for nothing as Kent lost, but it would never be forgotten by anyone who was there that day.

It was in the following year that he joined the ranks of the cricketing immortals. With their new brand of pinch-hitting, Sri Lanka lit up the World Cup and reached the final against Australia at Lahore. Australia were sitting pretty at 137-1 with their strong middle order of Steve Waugh, Stuart Law and Michael Bevan yet to come, but de Silva had other ideas. He spun his off breaks to take three wickets and pouched two catches to restrict Australia to a final total of 241-7.

His side were soon in trouble at 23-2 with both their swashbuckling openers gone, but he rebuilt the innings first with Asanka Gurusinha and then with his captain, Arjuna Ranatunga. He ended unbeaten on 107 as Sri Lanka won their first global crown, and his country was on the map for good, with de Silva the first to score a century and take three wickets in the same World Cup match – and still the only one to do so in the final.

Player	Batting	Bowling	Match	Venue	Year
P.A. de Silva	107*	3-42	Sri Lanka v Australia	Lahore	1996
J.F. Kloppenburg	121	4-42	Netherlands v Namibia	Bloemfontein	2003
S.T. Jayasuriya	115	3-38	Sri Lanka v West Indies	Providence	2007
T.M. Dilshan	144	4-4	Sri Lanka v Zimbabwe	Pallekele	2011

He started a love affair with the Sinhalese Sports Club, twice scoring twin centuries in a Test at the ground in 1997, and finally signed off from Test cricket in 2002 as one of only three players to score a double-century in his final innings.

Score	Player	Match	Venue	Year
258	S.M. Nurse	West Indies v New Zealand	Christchurch	1969
206	P.A. de Silva	Sri Lanka v Bangladesh	Colombo – PSS	2002
201*	J.N. Gillespie	Australia v Bangladesh	Chittagong – D	2006

Clyde Walcott   international career 1948–60

'I have never seen a more powerful batsman than Walcott, and when he was "going", it was almost impossible to bowl a length to him.' Richie Benaud

The youngest of the 'Three Ws' born close to Kensington Oval grew to be the biggest of the three and his game was characterised by power when most batsmen were characterised by 'touch' play. It wasn't just brute strength though, for he had the technique to back it up, and could defend solidly when required.

Clyde Walcott first played with Frank Worrell at the age of 12 for Combermere School and having subsequently moved to Harrison College, took up wicketkeeping as the school needed someone behind the stumps. He performed so well that he celebrated his sixteenth birthday by making his first-class debut for Barbados against Trinidad at Port of Spain. At the age of 20 he shared a world-record unbroken partnership of 574 with Worrell for the fourth wicket against Trinidad, and having scored 120 against the England tourists in early 1948, he was drafted into the Test side.

Still seen as a wicketkeeper who could bat, he did little to suggest anything else was the case as his top score in four Tests was just 45. However, it was a different story on the tour of India later that year when he struck two centuries in the same series in which Everton Weekes made four such scores.

And so to England, for the seminal 1950 tour. He stood up to the stumps for all 231 overs bowled by Ramadhin and Valentine at Lord's and struck an unbeaten 168 in the second innings to lead the West Indies to a famous victory. His next assignment jolted him back to reality, as Lindwall and Miller limited him to a total of just 87 runs in three Tests in Australia, and back trouble led to him giving up the wicketkeeping gloves for good.

His form returned during the home series with India in 1953, and he found England's bowling very much to his liking the following year when he struck 220 at Bridgetown, 124 at Port of Spain and 116 at Kingston. But that was merely a taste of things to come.

Shorn of his wicketkeeping duties, he exacted revenge on the Australian tourists who ventured to the Caribbean in early 1955. He started with a century in Jamaica and then struck two centuries at Trinidad, and two more when the action returned to Jamaica, to set a record for a series that has not been equalled since – and all those runs were made against a bowling attack featuring Miller, Lindwall, Benaud, Johnson and Johnston.

Player	Team	Against	Season	100s
C.L. Walcott	**West Indies**	**Australia**	**1954/55**	**5**
19 batsmen with				4

It was in this series that he also set a record – since equalled – for the highest ICC Test batting rating ever achieved by a West Indian batsman.

Player	Date	Points
C.L. Walcott	**Jun 1955**	**938**
G.S. Sobers	Jan 1967	**938**
I.V.A. Richards	Mar 1981	**938**
E.D. Weekes	Mar 1956	**927**
G.A. Headley	Jan 1948	**915**

The 1957 tour of England was a wholly different experience, and after starting with an innings of 90 at Edgbaston, he failed to pass 50 in the rest of the series. That experience helped hasten his retirement at the end of the 1958 series against Pakistan, and although he reappeared in two further Tests against England two years later, he dedicated himself to business after that.

He maintained close links with the game, first as a coach and then an administrator, helping to develop the careers of Rohan Kanhai and Clive Lloyd, among others. He was knighted for his services to the game and in 1993 was elected as chairman of the ICC.

Chapter 3

All-rounders

Garry Sobers   international career 1954–74

'To describe Sobers' method I would use the term lyrical. His immense power is concealed, or lightened, to the spectator's eye, by a rhythm which has in it as little obvious propulsion as a movement of music by Mozart.' Neville Cardus

Garry Sobers was the ultimate triple threat – with bat, ball or in the field. It could be said he was a quadruple threat as he could bowl both seam and spin to great effect. It wasn't just what he did on the field, but how he did it. For two decades he transcended the game – in an era that was ironically marked by some of the slowest periods of play in Test cricket.

Sobers was without doubt the finest batsman in the world over the course of his career – not to mention the greatest strokeplayer. To this day, no one has topped the ICC rankings for Test batsmen for more matches.

Player	Team	Matches
G.S. Sobers	**WI**	**189**
I.V.A. Richards	WI	**179**
S.P.D. Smith	Aus	**159**
B.C. Lara	WI	**140**
S.R. Tendulkar	Ind	**139**

If he was not the greatest bowler, he was certainly the most versatile, whether taking the new ball or spinning the older one either in an orthodox or unorthodox manner. In the field he could snap up half-chances with consummate ease and cover ground like a greyhound in the outfield.

At the time of his retirement, he was the leading run-scorer in Test cricket, with the highest individual score also to his name. His unbeaten innings of 365 against Pakistan not only eclipsed Len Hutton's all-time Test record, but it remains the highest maiden Test century ever scored.

He was also the second-highest wicket-taker for the West Indies, and third in the all-time list of catches taken in the field. And no one has ever scored more runs in a first-class over – and luckily, the TV cameras happened to be there to capture the moment forever.

Runs	Batsman	Bowler	Match	Venue	Year
36	**G.S. Sobers**	**M.A. Nash**	**Nottinghamshire v Glamorgan**	**Swansea**	**1968**
36	R.J. Shastri	Tilak Raj	Bombay v Baroda	Bombay	1985
34	E.B. Alletson	E.H. Killick	Nottinghamshire v Sussex	Hove	1911
34	F.C. Hayes	M.A. Nash	Lancashire v Glamorgan	Swansea	1977
34	A. Flintoff	A.J. Tudor	Lancashire v Surrey	Manchester	1998
34	C.M. Spearman	S.J.P. Moreton	Gloucestershire v Oxford UCCE	Oxford	2005

When he found himself playing in Kuala Lumpur in March 1964, he took five wickets in five balls for E.W. Swanton's XI against Malaysia.

Many of his numbers have subsequently been overtaken, but the world has not seen his like again. There were tales of late-night drinking sessions only ending when he had to stride to the crease for the following day's play. He scored 251 in a Sheffield Shield match in Adelaide, which ended on 13 February 1962. He then hopped on a plane – well, three planes, actually – and undertook fifty-five hours of travel to arrive the night before a Test match against India at Port of Spain, which started on 16 February. He then proceeded to take six wickets in the match and score 40 in his only innings. And modern-day cricketers moan about their workloads!

He lit up the famous Brisbane Tied Test of 1960, with an innings of 132, and on the 1966 Test tour of England he scored 722 runs, took twenty wickets and held ten catches – all while captaining the side. Showing how far he was ahead of his time, in 1967 he authored a book entitled *Bonaventure and the Flashing Blade* – a children's novel in which computer analysis helps a university cricket team become unbeatable. Nowadays you would be hard pushed to find any professional team that does not perform statistical analysis using computers.

Off the field he was equally adept on the golf course, where he played off scratch, or in the casino, where he was a prolific bettor.

Jacques Kallis   **international career 1995–2014**

'I truly believe he is the best cricketer ever. He is truly phenomenal.' Kevin Pietersen

In years to come, those of us who watched international cricket in the 1990s and 2000s will look back in awe at this colossus of a player who – despite his startling feats – was seemingly unappreciated and underrated at the time. To this day, no one has spent more matches worldwide as the top-ranked all-rounder in the ICC Test rankings than he did.

Player	Team	Matches
J.H. Kallis	**SA**	**493**
G.S. Sobers	WI	**213**
Shakib Al Hasan	Ban	**175**
K.R. Miller	Aus	**134**
R.J. Hadlee	NZ	**133**

Wynberg Boys' High School in Cape Town is the second-oldest school in South Africa and has a reputation of being a finishing school for South African sporting excellence. It says something that their cricket field was renamed the 'Jacques Kallis Oval' in honour of their greatest sporting son.

He was without doubt one of the best batsmen of his era – one in which he shared the limelight with Ponting, Lara and Tendulkar. However, when all had taken their sweaters and ridden off into the sunset, Kallis' batting average outstripped the lot of them.

He was less prolific with the ball than the bat, but he gave the South African team a perfect balance and the ability to always play an extra batsman knowing that he could contribute with the ball. His bowling lost some of its earlier penetration later in his career, but he was still capable of bowling destructive spells, and he was a slip catcher of nonchalant brilliance. Thanks to his orthodoxy with both bat and ball, he was able to keep injury-free for most of his career, and had great control of his emotions, except for when appealing vigorously for a wicket.

It was a slowish start, though, with just one century and a batting average of 25.37 in his first sixteen Tests, but it was the 1998 tour of England that first marked him out for greatness. He took 4-29 at Lord's and followed up with 132 at Manchester, showing what a double threat he could be on the greatest stage. That same year, he helped South Africa win the inaugural ICC Champions Trophy – still the only major trophy in their cabinet. He hit 113 in the semi-final before taking 5-30 against the West Indies in the final.

Once assured of his place in the Test team, records started to fall. In late 2001, he batted for 1,240 minutes between dismissals, scoring 456 runs in the process. Two years later, he stroked centuries in five successive Tests and went even better in 2007, scoring five centuries over the course of just four matches.

The detractors would point to his sluggish scoring rate, but his technique was more textbook than some of his more flamboyant contemporaries. He did not have Lara's flourish or Ponting's trademark pull, or the cavalier attitude of Sehwag. However, in ODI cricket he worked hard to develop his game and flourished in the early years of the Indian Premier League.

He became more of a reluctant bowler as his years advanced, but over the same time his batting feats entered the stratosphere, finally cracking that elusive double-century at the thirty-eighth time of asking. He left on a high, too, with an innings of 115 in his final Test in the 2013 Durban Boxing Day match against India, and ended with more Player of the Match awards than any other Test cricketer.

Player	Team	Matches	MOM
J.H. Kallis	SA	166	23
M. Muralitharan	SL	133	19
Wasim Akram	Pak	104	17
S.K. Warne	Aus	145	17
K.C. Sangakara	SL	134	16
R.T. Ponting	Aus	168	16

W.G. Grace   international career 1880–99

'He revolutionised cricket. He turned it from an accomplishment into a science.'
K.S. Ranjitsinhji

As W.G. Grace strode off the first-class cricket field for the last time at The Oval in August 1908 at the age of 60, here is how the leading run-scorers, wicket-takers and catchers stood at the time:

Player	Runs	Player	Wickets	Player	Catches
W.G. Grace	54,211	W.G. Grace	2,809	W.G. Grace	874
R. Abel	33,128	J.T. Hearne	2,502	J. Tunnicliffe	695

W.G. looms large over cricket history, with his huge girth and unparalleled beard, and it sometimes becomes difficult to look past this figure and examine his feats on the cricket field. Taking each of those tables in isolation, it would point to Grace being the dominant player of that era, but taking them all together gives some idea of the giant he was in the formative years of the game.

In Victorian life he was the most recognised person, outside the Royal Family and Prime Minister Gladstone, and even now, more than a hundred years after his death, he is the possessor of the most famous beard in sport. He was the first global sporting superstar and possibly the only one until Babe Ruth started hitting baseballs out of ballparks at an alarming rate in the 1920s. He dominated cricket all the way from the village green to Lord's, and cricket entered the national epoch in no small part thanks to him.

He established himself as a master batsman at the age of just 16 and his dominance can be seen from examining the national averages in 1871. Grace hit 2,739 runs at the unheard-of average of 78.90. Next on the list came Richard Daft, who averaged 37 in scoring his 565 runs. In 1876, Grace scored 344 for MCC against Kent, 177 for Gloucestershire against Nottinghamshire, and then 318 not out against Yorkshire – all in the space of a week.

Sceptics could point to the fact that he never had to play against the fastest of bowling, or against reverse swing or combat the googly. However, he had to contend with longer boundaries, far worse wickets and exhausting travel schedules, not to mention a demanding job away from cricket.

He started bowling round-arm at medium pace and slowed as he became older, but what he lacked in pace he made up for with subtle guile and flight. Added to all of this, he was an excellent fielder – mainly at point – where he could chat to the batsman and employ an early style of gamesmanship to try to gain any advantage possible.

All the while, he maintained his role as a doctor, frequently visiting friends after a hard day in the field to try to lift their spirits and alleviate pain. In 1887, Gloucestershire's Arthur Croome gashed his throat against one of the spiked railings in front of the pavilion at Old Trafford and the cut was deep and potentially fatal. Grace held the edges of the wound together for nearly half an hour as messengers found surgical needles.

We can never be certain whether he replaced the bails and kept on batting, claiming that the hordes of people had not turned up to see the bowler but to see him bat. Or that he called 'The lady' when tossing the coin so that he could claim victory whether it landed on Queen Victoria or Britannia. He played within the rules but was keen to stretch them to the limits. His final innings in any cricket was for Eltham against Grove Park in July 1914, when the winds of war were already blowing. Needless to say, he top-scored with 69 not out. Later that summer he wrote a letter to *The Sportsman*, willing cricketers to 'put bat and ball away and come to the help of their country without delay in its hour of need'.

Somewhat fittingly, this icon of British life in the second half of the nineteenth century died during the war that marked the end of Britain's empire. And when – in 1923 – the decision was made about how to commemorate him on the gates at Lord's that bear his name, he was described as: 'William Gilbert Grace – the Great Cricketer'. That summed him up.

Imran Khan   international career 1971–92

'When Imran was captain, there was never a question of anyone else being in charge. And that more than anything, won them the 1992 World Cup.' Tony Greig

When does a player become a legend? And when does a legend become an icon? Imran Khan transcended cricket in a way few others could. When he retired after the 1987 World Cup, President Zia-ul-Haq asked him to reconsider, and he did so, culminating with lifting the trophy in 1992.

He was born into cricket royalty as his mother was from the Burki Pashtun tribe who settled in Jalandhar and produced several other cricketers, the most prominent of whom were his cousins Javed Burki and Majid Khan – both of whom also captained Pakistan.

He made his Test debut as an 18-year-old on the 1971 tour of England, before he was accepted to study Politics, Philosophy and Economics at Keble College, Oxford. It was a course that would serve him well later in life. After graduating in 1975, he initially struggled in international cricket before a twelve-wicket haul at Sydney in January 1977 propelled him to stardom.

He signed for Kerry Packer's World Series Cricket, where he finished third in a fast bowling contest at Perth, only behind Jeff Thomson and Michael Holding, and ahead of Dennis Lillee and Andy Roberts. He also took advantage of his time there, taking advice from Mike Procter on his run-up and John Snow on how best to position his shoulder at the moment of delivery.

He reached the peak of his powers in 1982, topping both batting and bowling averages in Pakistan's series in England, before taking forty wickets at just 13.95 apiece in six Tests against India to reach the highest ICC Test Bowling Rating by anyone since the First World War.

Player	Team	Month	Points
Imran Khan	**Pak**	**Jan 1983**	**922**
M. Muralitharan	SL	Jul 2007	**920**
G.D. McGrath	Aus	Aug 2001	**914**
P.J. Cummins	Aus	Aug 2019	**914**
G.A.R. Lock	Eng	Jul 1958	**912**
C.E.L. Ambrose	WI	Mar 1994	**912**
V.D. Philander	SA	Dec 2013	**912**

However, he suffered a stress fracture to his shin, and only experimental treatment funded by the Pakistan government helped him back to full fitness.

It was he who inspired Pakistani youngsters to bowl quickly despite the flat wickets in their home country. It was he who encouraged a huge following for his national team. And it was he who transformed a group of talented – but mercurial – cricketers into an international force to be reckoned with and one capable on their day of holding their own with the mighty West Indies sides of the 1980s.

Of the four great all-rounders of his generation, Imran was the one whose talents did not diminish with age. He kept scoring runs and never stopped taking wickets, as his final batting and bowling average will testify.

Player	Team	Bat avge	Bowl avge	Bat/Bowl
Imran Khan	**Pak**	**37.69**	**22.81**	**1.65**
R.J. Hadlee	NZ	27.16	22.29	**1.22**
I.T. Botham	Eng	33.54	28.40	**1.18**
Kapil Dev	Ind	31.05	29.64	**1.05**

He was the perfect combination of supreme cricketing talent and film-star good looks. Statistics do not show him to be the best captain Pakistan ever had, but he was certainly the most charismatic.

Having captained his country to World Cup glory, he promptly retired from the game – this time for good. But he was never going to fade away quietly. He set about raising money for a cancer hospital in his mother's name and launched himself on the political stage, which culminated in August 2018 when he was elected Pakistan's twenty-second prime minister. His appeal is seemingly timeless.

Ian Botham   international career 1976–92

'He doesn't give a damn; he wants to ride a horse, down a pint, roar around the land, waking up the sleepers, show them things can be done.' Peter Roebuck

England's greatest modern-day all-rounder at his peak hit heights that very few cricketers have ever done. He won five Ashes series – a modern-day record – sometimes off his own back. When England cried out for a hero, Ian Botham stepped into the breech, frequently setting grounds alight and emptying bars with both bat and ball.

Born in Cheshire, his family moved south to Yeovil when his father obtained a job with Westland Helicopters. Educated at Buckler's Mead Secondary Modern School in Yeovil, seldom was he home from school before 8.00 pm, his time taken up with all manner of sporting activities. At the age of 15 he was faced with a choice. The Crystal Palace manager, Bert Head, had shown some interest in signing the young Botham, but Somerset sent him to Lord's, where he was offered a groundstaff contract.

The public first became aware of his never-say-die attitude in a Benson & Hedges Cup quarter-final against Hampshire at Taunton in 1974. Somerset were struggling at 113-8 chasing an unlikely 183 to win. Shortly after arriving at the crease, Botham was felled by an Andy Roberts bouncer, which knocked out four of his teeth. Undaunted, he opted to carry on, and struck an unbeaten 45 to lead his side home by one wicket and make his first appearance on the front pages of the newspapers he was to grace on so many occasions.

His early international career was breathtaking. He took just twenty-one matches to achieve the 1,000 run/100 wicket double in Test cricket, which is still a record.

Player	Team	Matches
I.T. Botham	**Eng**	**21**
M.H. Mankad	Ind	23
R. Ashwin	Ind	24
Kapil Dev	Ind	25
S.M. Pollock	SA	26

His feats in the Mumbai heat in the Golden Jubilee Test in February 1980 were extraordinary. Bowling an unbroken spell of twenty-six overs throughout India's second innings, he became the first player to score a century and take at least ten wickets in the same Test.

Player	Batting	Bowling	Match	Venue	Year
I.T. Botham	**114**	**6-58 & 7-48**	**England v India**	**Mumbai**	**1980**
Imran Khan	117	6-98 & 5-82	Pakistan v India	Faisalabad	1983
Shakib Al Hasan	137 & 6	5-80 & 5-44	Bangladesh v Zimbabwe	Khulna	2014

After twenty-five Tests, his batting average stood at 40.48 and his bowling average 18.52. Despite slowing down later in his career, he remains the record holder in terms of the fewest matches taken to reach both the 2,000 run/200 wicket and 3,000 run/300 wicket double.

With the bat he struck fourteen Test centuries, and to put that into perspective, the combined talents of Imran, Kapil and Hadlee hit sixteen between them. Both James Anderson and Stuart Broad have surpassed his then national record of 383 Test wickets, but it took Anderson 151 Tests to better Botham's twenty-seven five-wicket hauls that came in his 102 Tests.

If he was already world class, the much-chronicled 1981 Ashes series elevated him to superstardom. Having started the series in the depths of despair with defeat at Trent Bridge and a 'pair' at Lord's, he roared back and almost single-handedly won three Tests in that series. His feats with both bat and ball elevated him to tabloid hero status and everything that came with that.

He was never quite the same again, as his back gave way, and despite occasional flashes of brilliance, he ended his international career a pale shadow of the man who had set the cricketing world alight a decade earlier.

Few in the history of cricket have hit the ball harder, bowled the ball faster, and caught the ball better than Botham did in his prime. And he remained a country boy at heart, never happier than walking his dogs or fishing for those elusive salmon. Equally at home with both the famous and the general British public, more than a quarter of a century after leaving the international arena, he remained the biggest name in English cricket.

Keith Miller   **international career 1946–56**

'If Keith had had the same outlook as Bradman or Ponsford, he would have made colossal scores. He could, if he desired, have become the statisticians' greatest customer.' Sid Barnes

Austerity was the way of life after the Second World War and perhaps unsurprisingly for someone who had served in it with such distinction, Keith Miller flew in the face of such adversity.

In his childhood, Miller aspired to become a jockey, but that career choice was thwarted when he suddenly underwent a growth spurt of 28 centimetres at the age of 16. That put an end to his riding career, but he maintained an active interest in racing for the rest of his life, later working for Vernons Pools.

His cricketing talent was discovered by his high school geometry teacher, Bill Woodfull – himself a former Ashes winning captain. He was a classical batsman with elegant drives and effortless pulls, and with the ball he possessed a high action, and could move the ball both ways at pace. Soon he was making his first-class debut – hitting 181 – but shortly afterwards, war broke out.

Miller had been born halfway through the pioneering flight from England to Australia by aviators Keith and Ross Smith in 1919, and as befitted a man given their names, he earned his wings in the Royal Australian Air Force in late 1942. Flying an assortment of Beauforts, Beaufighters and Mosquitos, he had several near-misses and cheated death on a number of occasions. He undertook missions over Germany in April and May 1945, and when invited to fly over Germany post-surrender, he broke away from the rest of the formation in order to fly over Bonn – Beethoven's birthplace. For such a lover of classical music, any trip over Germany would have seemed incomplete without paying such respects.

Michael Parkinson asked him many years later about pressure in cricket, to which he responded with his famous quote: 'Pressure is a Messerschmitt up your arse, playing cricket is not.'

Once the war in Europe was over, Miller played in the 'Victory Tests' against England in 1945 for a team of Australian servicemen who happened to be in England at the time. He scored two centuries against England and then struck 185 in less than three hours for the Dominions – a side captained by Learie Constantine – against an England side at Lord's in late August.

He played a crucial role on the 1948 'Invincibles' tour of England as Bradman's team were unbeaten in all thirty-four of their matches, and carried on throughout the early 1950s performing great feats with both bat and ball. Frequently batting as high as number three, he scored three Ashes centuries and four against the West Indies, and ended his career with by far the best ratio of batting average to bowling average of any Australian in Test history, with a minimum of 2,000 runs and 100 wickets.

Player	Bat avge	Bowl avge	Bat/Bowl
K.R. Miller	**36.97**	**22.97**	1.61
R. Benaud	24.45	27.03	**0.90**
M.G. Johnson	22.20	28.40	**0.78**
S.K. Warne	17.32	25.41	**0.68**

Even greater than his feats on the field were the tales off it. There is the story of Bradman answering a knock on the door late one night to see Miller dressed in a dinner suit, informing him that he had been in bed at curfew as demanded and was going out now that the rules had been met. In November 1955, he arrived at the Sydney Cricket Ground for the second day's play captaining New South Wales, still wearing his dinner suit from the previous evening. He then proceeded to set the field with the single command: 'Scatter', before taking seven wickets to bowl South Australia out for 27.

On his final tour of England at the age of 36, with Ray Lindwall out injured, he became the first Australian bowler for more than half a century – and just the third in all – to take ten wickets in a Lord's Test.

Bowling	Player	Year
10-63	C.T.B. Turner	1888
10-164	E. Jones	1899
10-152	**K.R. Miller**	**1956**
16-137	R.A.L. Massie	1972

As great as his statistical feats were, his contribution to the post-war Australian team was even greater. He is remembered to this day as much for his personality as for being as much of a crowd favourite as anyone who has ever played the game. He was a true 'Boy's Own' hero.

Wilfred Rhodes   **international career 1899–1930**

'When George Hirst got you out, you were out. When Wilfred got you out, you were out twice, because he knew by then how to get you out in the second innings.'
Roy Kilner

Neville Cardus summed him up perfectly: 'He was Yorkshire cricket personified.' Wilfred Rhodes was a superb all-rounder, ending just 31 runs short of an astonishing 40,000 run/4,000 wicket first-class double. He took a total of 4,204 first-class wickets – the most in history – gathered over a career stretching from 1898 to 1930.

He hailed from the same Yorkshire town of Kirkheaton that gave us George Hirst; the two Yorkshiremen carried England to victory in the famous 1902 Test at The Oval and were instrumental in many domestic triumphs when they were not plying their trade in international cricket. For such a small place with a population of less than 4,000 to produce two such players was quite remarkable.

He first appeared for Yorkshire in 1898 and was soon into his stride, ending his debut season with a tally of 154 wickets at an average of 14.60 apiece – good enough for second place in the national averages. He also contributed three 50s with the bat, starting to show some of the skill that would enable him to perform the domestic 'double' of 1,000 runs and 100 wickets in a season on more occasions than anyone else.

Player	'Doubles'
W. Rhodes	**16**
G.H. Hirst	**14**
V.W.C. Jupp	**10**

Rhodes bowled with the perfect combination of a high arm and immaculate flight and length, able to extract any assistance from the pitch if it were forthcoming. He was also meticulous in setting – and bowling to – his field. On a good wicket he was difficult to score off, but on a tricky one he was lethal. Never was his skill more demonstrated than in the Melbourne Test of 1904, when he took 7-56 and 8-68 to spin England to a memorable victory.

Starting his international career as a genuine tail-ender, on the 1903/04 tour of Australia his captain Pelham Warner wanted him to concentrate exclusively on his bowling, and so he rarely batted higher than ninth in the order. At Sydney, he made an unbeaten 40 out of a last wicket partnership of 130 with 'Tip' Foster, which remains England's Ashes record to this day.

After that tour he rose to the giddy heights of opener, becoming one of the select band of men to have batted in every position in the order in Test cricket. In 1911, he found himself in Australia again, this time as opening partner to Jack Hobbs. In the Fourth Test at Melbourne, they added 323 for England's first wicket, which also remains an Ashes record.

He was already 41 when cricket resumed after the First World War but he showed no signs of slowing down for Yorkshire, even if his Test returns tailed off. However, there remained one glorious final effort when he was recalled for the final match in the 1926 Ashes series at the age of 48. The series was 0-0 with just the Oval Test to play and his inclusion was met with a great deal of surprise. However, it was fully justified as he took 4-44 in Australia's second innings to seal victory and the series.

Having started his Test career in W.G. Grace's final match, he ended it when the supremacy of Don Bradman had already been established, enjoying the longest Test career of them all.

Player	Team	Career length
W. Rhodes	**Eng**	**30y 315d**
D.B. Close	Eng	**26y 356d**
F.E. Woolley	Eng	**25y 13d**
G.A. Headley	WI	**24y 10d**
S.R. Tendulkar	Ind	**24y 1d**

Mike Procter   international career 1967–70

'There have been few better all-round cricketers in the world in my time.' Sir Garfield Sobers

Gloucestershire has had many great players – from the Graces to Jessop to Hammond to Graveney and to Zaheer Abbas, but only once was the county identified with just one man, and he was a man from South Africa.

Starting out as a wicketkeeper batsman, Mike Proctor hit five centuries for Highbury School in the 1959 season, which included an unbeaten 210 against Transvaal Schools. He only started bowling when he was older and had become stronger, soon developing his 'wrong foot' bowling action, which enabled him to swing the ball prodigiously. A natural athlete, he was his school's fly half and represented them at hockey, tennis, squash and athletics.

In the mid-1960s, there were no overseas players in county cricket as qualification depended on living in the country for eighteen months. And so, in 1965, two young South Africans, Barry Richards and Mike Procter, spent a summer playing for Gloucestershire Second XI. Needless to say, they topped the batting and bowling averages, but it was Procter who topped the batting and Richards the bowling! When the qualification rules were dropped three years later, Richards signed for Hampshire and Procter returned to the West Country.

Procter could smash the fastest of centuries before wreaking havoc among opposition batsmen with the ball by bowling pace or sharply turning spin. Two of his four hat-tricks were entirely claimed lbw and twice for the county he scored a century and took a hat-trick in the same first-class match – a record only equalled more than thirty years later.

Player	Matches	Years
Mike Procter	**2**	**1972, 1979**
Sohag Gazi	2	2012, 2013
12 others	1	

Early in his career he equalled a world record by striking centuries in six successive first-class innings, which culminated in a career-best innings of 254 for Rhodesia against Western Province.

He inspired Gloucestershire to triumphs in the Gillette Cup in 1973 and the Benson & Hedges Cup four years later, a tournament in which he took four wickets in five balls in the semi-final victory over Hampshire at Southampton. What wickets they were – Gordon Greenidge, Barry Richards, Trevor Jesty and John Rice – all without any help from a fielder. He also struck six successive sixes off Somerset's Dennis Breakwell, and hence Gloucestershire became Proctershire.

Alas, his Test career was cut short due to circumstances beyond his control. But like his contemporary, Richards, he had started in a blaze of glory, taking forty-one wickets in his seven Tests at a scarcely believable average of 15.02. When the 1970 South African tour of England was cancelled, he represented the 'Rest of the World' in five matches against England, played with all the trappings and intensity of Test matches. He scored 292 runs at an average of 48.66, and his fifteen wickets cost just 23.93 runs apiece. It was the closest he came to playing Test cricket against England.

After that, his talents were almost exclusively limited to English and South African domestic cricket. His only further international recognition was in World Series Cricket in the late 1970s, when he more than made his mark. He could console himself with ending his career with more first-class wickets than any other South African.

Player	Matches	Wickets	Avge
M.J. Procter	**401**	**1,417**	**19.53**
A.A. Donald	316	**1,216**	22.76
C.B. Llewellyn	267	**1,013**	23.41
C.E.B. Rice	482	**930**	22.49
H.J. Tayfield	187	**864**	25.91

Had he played international cricket, his career would have overlapped the start of the careers of the great all-rounders of the 1980s, but while they flourished on the international stage, Procter's feats were kept somewhat in the shade. What a team the South Africans could have had in those times.

Aubrey Faulkner   **international career 1906–24**

'The yardstick for assessing a great all-rounder is whether or not he could play Test cricket purely as a batsman or purely as a bowler. Faulkner was unquestionably one of the rare breed.' Brian Bassano

In recent times, South African cricket has been blessed with more than its fair share of all-round talent. In Brian McMillan, Jacques Kallis and Shaun Pollock, they boasted three of the finest. However, only one player has ever topped both ICC batting and bowling rankings in Test cricket, and that man was Aubrey Faulkner.

Playing for the weakest of the three international teams at the time, he lost a great deal of playing time due to the First World War, but his statistics still withstand the test of time as he could have held his place in the team as either a batsman or a bowler.

South Africa had much the worse of the earlier skirmishes in Test cricket with England and lost each of the first eight Test matches between the sides. However, all that changed in the 1905/06 season as Faulkner helped inspire them to a 4-1 series victory, taking fourteen wickets at 19.42 apiece.

He was a part of the famous googly quartet that lifted and characterised South African cricket in that first decade of the twentieth century, together with Reggie Schwarz, Bert Vogler and Gordon White, and all four of them debuted in the first match of that triumphant 1905/06 series.

He was even better on England's next tour, scoring 545 runs and taking twenty-nine wickets in the five Tests as the series was won 3-2. With the bat, his star shone brightest in the 1910/11 series in Australia, when the hosts were put to the sword to the tune of 732 runs in the five matches, including a career-best innings of 204 in the Second Test at Melbourne. That was the first double-century ever scored by a South African batsman in Test cricket and would remain the only one until Dudley Nourse scored 231 against Australia at Johannesburg a quarter of a century later.

When he scored an unbeaten 122 for South Africa against Australia at Old Trafford in the opening match of the 1912 Triangular series in England, he became the first batsman to score at least a hundred runs in seven successive Test matches, a mark only equalled nearly a century later.

Matches	Player	Team	Years
7	**G.A. Faulkner**	SA	1910–12
7	G. Gambhir	Ind	2008–10
6	D.G. Bradman	Aus	1937–38
6	A.D. Nourse	SA	1939–47
6	J.H. Kallis	SA	2003–04

In the so-called 'Golden Age of Cricket', which ran from 1890–1914, Faulkner was one of only five players to score more than a thousand runs and take more than fifty wickets in Test cricket, and his performances compared incredibly favourably with his peers.

Player	Team	Bat Avge	Bowl Avge	Bat/Bowl
G.A. Faulkner	SA	41.87	25.52	1.64
W. Rhodes	Eng	33.56	24.71	1.35
M.A. Noble	Aus	27.70	25.10	1.10
W.W. Armstrong	Aus	35.66	35.81	0.99
J.H. Sinclair	SA	23.23	31.68	0.73

Enlisting in the British Army, he served on the Western Front and in Macedonia, Egypt and Palestine. His bravery earned him the Distinguished Service Order and the Order of the Nile, despite contracting malaria. Faulkner was recalled to play for South Africa in response to an injury crisis on their 1924 tour of England, but he was past his best, and after one disappointing performance at Lord's, he retired for good.

That wasn't the end of his cricket, as he opened a cricket school in London – first operating out of a garage in Richmond, before finding larger premises in Walham Green. He could name Doug Wright, Ian Peebles and Tom Killick as some of the youngsters whose games he helped to shape for future successes.

Alas, his story has a tragic ending, as he suffered from prolonged bouts of depression and ended up taking his own life in September 1930.

Chapter 4

Wicketkeepers

Adam Gilchrist   international career 1996–2008

'He was the one guy that went out and changed the wicketkeeping mould for all of us.' Kumar Sangakkara

Before Adam Gilchrist came along, wicketkeepers were supposed to bat around seven or eight in the order and were traditionally pugnacious types who fought it out. Gilchrist changed not only that view but also the view of wicketkeepers ever since.

He received his first pair of wicketkeeping gloves at the age of 10 and reached a crossroads seven years later when he had to choose between taking university entrance exams or travelling on a cricket scholarship to England. He chose the latter, and spent a summer playing for Richmond in the Middlesex League.

Having cut his teeth in the same Australian Under-19 side as Damien Martyn, he moved west from his native New South Wales to Western Australia in search of securing his place in a state side. That he managed, and international honours came two years later in the ODI side, and he helped Australia to win the first of three successive World Cups in 1999.

There were murmurs of discontent when he replaced a legend in Ian Healy behind the stumps for Australia in Test cricket, but these were soon forgotten once he had hit 81 on debut and a thrilling, match-winning unbeaten 149 against Pakistan at Hobart in his next match to seal an improbable victory against the odds.

His keeping wasn't quite in the same league as Healy's, but he did have Shane Warne and Stuart MacGill to deal with for most of his international career. He more than made up for it with game-changing efforts with the bat, putting himself in the world-class all-rounder league. He was superb at understanding a game's situation, and either sticking it out through the tough situations, or taking it by the scruff of the neck, as he so often did.

It wasn't just the runs he scored but the way he scored them. Equally adept opening the innings in ODI cricket or at his familiar number seven spot for the Test side, no one had scored as many runs as quickly as he did. He became the first batsman to hit 100 sixes in Test cricket as well as winning three World Cups with Australia. In the 2007 final against Sri Lanka at Barbados, he smashed 149 from just 104 deliveries – the highest individual score in a World Cup final.

Score	Player	Match	Venue	Year
149	**A.C. Gilchrist**	**Australia v Sri Lanka**	**Bridgetown**	**2007**
140*	R.T. Ponting	Australia v India	Johannesburg	2003
138*	I.V.A. Richards	West Indies v England	Lord's	1979
107*	P.A. de Silva	Sri Lanka v Australia	Lahore	1996
103*	D.P.M.D. Jayawardene	Sri Lanka v India	Mumbai	2011
102	C.H. Lloyd	West Indies v Australia	Lord's	1975

Other records fell to his flashing blade. He failed by one delivery to equal Viv Richards' then record fifty-six-ball Test century at Perth in 2006; he was briefly the scorer of the fastest Test double-century; and he ended his career with more runs than any other Test wicketkeeper in history.

Player	Team	Runs	Avge
A.C. Gilchrist	**Aus**	**5,570**	**47.60**
M.V. Boucher	SA	**5,515**	30.30
MS Dhoni	Ind	**4,876**	38.09
A.J. Stewart	Eng	**4,540**	34.92
A. Flower	Zim	**4,404**	53.70

Above all of this he came across as a likeable, accessible hero – the country boy made good. He 'walked' when given not out in a World Cup semi-final and always seemed to play with a smile on his face. Before Gilchrist, a batting keeper was a luxury; after him, it became a necessity. He changed the complexion of wicketkeeping – especially in Test cricket – forever.

Kumar Sangakkara   international career 2000–15

'He was a very good violin player; and if he didn't play cricket, he would have been an outstanding tennis player.' Ranjit Fernando

It says something for Kumar Sangakkara that he was not named the 'Outstanding Schoolboy Cricketer' in Sri Lanka, but the 'Outstanding Schoolboy'. He was a chorister and talented violinist, and oozed charm from every pore.

Whereas his left-handed predecessors in the Sri Lankan team, Arjuna Ranatunga and Asanka Gurusinha, gave the impression they were up for a fight, Sangakkara was grace personified. Had he never even picked up the wicketkeeping gloves, he would be difficult to leave out of any team on pure batsmanship alone.

He started training as a lawyer at the University of Colombo, but the Bar's loss was cricket's gain, as he used his verbal skills to great effect to get under the skin of batsmen from behind the stumps. He promised to complete his degree after retirement, and who would argue with him, as it was not his style to leave things unfinished. At the age of 33 and still playing, he was invited to deliver the MCC's 'Spirit of Cricket' lecture at Lord's. He was just as at ease taking on the world's fiercest bowlers as he was representing his country on the world stage.

At Colombo in July 2006, he ground South Africa into the dust, sharing a first-class record partnership of 624 with his partner in crime Mahela Jayawardene, on whose shoulders so much of the batting burden for Sri Lanka was shared over so many years. It was no toothless bowling attack – consisting of Ntini, Steyn, Nel, Hall and Boje.

In a career of great moments, his unbeaten half-century to win ICC Men's T20 World Cup 2014 after his team had suffered so many near misses was probably the crowning glory. His 319 and 105 in a match against Bangladesh at Chittagong two months earlier helped him towards a record-breaking haul of international runs in any calendar year.

Player	Team	Year	Matches	Runs
K.C. Sangakkara	**SL**	**2014**	**48**	**2,868**
R.T. Ponting	Aus	2005	46	**2,833**
V. Kohli	Ind	2017	46	**2,818**
V. Kohli	Ind	2018	37	**2,735**
K.S. Williamson	NZ	2015	39	**2,692**

He became the most prolific run-scorer his country had ever known, with double-hundreds flowing from his bat with consummate ease. At the age of 37, he was still good enough to reel off four consecutive centuries in the 2015 World Cup, setting a new record.

Not for Sangakkara the fading away at the end of a long career. Having signed for Surrey at the start of 2015, he announced that 2017 would be his final season of first-class cricket. He then proceeded to score five successive centuries and fell just 16 runs short of joining C.B. Fry, Don Bradman and Mike Procter in scoring six in a row. For good measure, he then rattled off 180 not out, 164 and 157 in a row later in the season to sign off with the greatest ten-match run to end a first-class career in history.

Player	Runs	Avge	100s
K.C. Sangakkara	**1,491**	**106.50**	**8**
J.R.M. Mackay	**1,149**	76.60	5
J.J. Crowe	**1,063**	62.52	4
R.T. Ponting	**1,061**	70.73	4
C.L. Badcock	**1,060**	66.25	5

Alan Knott   international career 1967–81

'I think he is the most gifted and dedicated cricketer one could ever wish to play with, never satisfied with his performance and always seeking for a little more perfection.' Colin Cowdrey

Kent have been fortunate throughout their history to have had some of the most talented keepers in English cricket history. From Frederick Huish to Les Ames to Godfrey Evans, Alan Knott was the natural successor, and he kept with sustained brilliance for the county for twenty years.

For those twenty years, he became intrinsically linked to Derek Underwood, with 197 batsmen lured to their doom by the combination in 443 first-class matches together. They are now both immortalised at the county ground at Canterbury by lending their names to a stand, joining other former Kent legends Les Ames and Frank Woolley.

It could all have been so different, as he was advised as a small boy to bowl spin by Kent's coach and developed both off and leg breaks. But keeping was in his blood as his father had been a talented club wicketkeeper, and so practices at home soon took on a different form.

Like so many keepers, he was an eccentric – he was said to have stuffed raw steaks into his wicketkeeping gloves to add extra cushioning from the hard cricket ball and he also used to wrap his legs in a duvet while driving so that they kept warm. However, his infectious enthusiasm in the field could lift the spirits of his teammates on even the dullest of days. In the winter he trained regularly with Charlton Athletic and he also spent hours playing table tennis to maintain his reflexes.

His batting was a bonus. Unorthodox, with an excellent cut stroke, he could also use his feet to great effect against the spinners. He could be determined in a crisis, but also flamboyant enough a player to win the Walter Lawrence Trophy for the fastest first-class century in the 1976 English season by reaching three figures in just seventy minutes for Kent against Sussex at Canterbury.

For a decade from 1967 to 1977, he was a permanent fixture in the England team, at one stage setting a record of sixty-five successive Test appearances, which stood as the national record for nearly forty years and still ranks third on the all-time England list – an incredible achievement for a wicketkeeper.

Player	From	Until	Matches
A.N. Cook	May 2006	Sep 2018	159
J.E. Root	Jun 2014	Jan 2020	77
A.P.E. Knott	**Mar 1971**	**Aug 1977**	**65**
I.T. Botham	Feb 1978	Mar 1984	65
M.A. Atherton	Feb 1993	Aug 1998	63

When England regained the Ashes in 1970/71, Knott was pivotal in the triumph, with five catches and a stumping in the decisive Seventh Test match at Sydney. His captain, Ray Illingworth, remarked that it was not possible to keep better than Knott had in that series. As Lillee and Thomson pulverised the English batsmen on their tour of Australia four years later, Knott stood fearlessly against the onslaught, scoring 364 runs in the Tests with three 50s and 106 at Adelaide.

He played another key role in the 1977 Ashes triumph. Striding to the wicket at Nottingham with England struggling at 82/5 in reply to Australia's first-innings total of 243, he struck a career-best 135, helping England to reach 364 and an eventual seven-wicket triumph.

When his international career ended, he had made more dismissals than any other England wicketkeeper, despite the fact that he missed the best part of three years with the international side having chosen to play World Series Cricket with his former captain, Tony Greig.

Player	Matches	Dismissals
A.P.E. Knott	**95**	**269**
M.J. Prior	79	**256**
A.J. Stewart	82	**241**
T.G. Evans	91	**219**
J.M. Bairstow	49	**184**

Andy Flower   international career 1992–2003

'He's pulled us out of a number of tough situations and always been the benchmark for the team.' Heath Streak

Born into a sport-loving family in Cape Town, Andy Flower's family settled in Zimbabwe when he was 10, and he was soon posting huge scores for North Park School. He only took up wicketkeeping at the age of 15, when his speculative off breaks became less successful, and he made his first-class debut three years later.

After leaving school he found work in finance, but always hoped to receive an offer to play cricket abroad, which eventually came from Barnt Green in the Birmingham League. In his early days, he also plied his trade for Heywood in the Central Lancashire League, and for Voorburg in the Netherlands.

What he lacked in natural talent he more than made up for with grit, determination and an undying will to succeed. His first international appearance came against Sri Lanka in the 1992 World Cup and it was to sum up his career perfectly. He anchored his side's innings, batting through all fifty overs to score an unbeaten 115. It wasn't enough though, as Arjuna Ranatunga led Sri Lanka home in the final over.

His runs never came easily, made as they were with his team's back often up against the wall and without another truly world-class player in his side. Unsurprisingly, he rates his innings of 156 against Pakistan at Harare in 1995 his best, as it helped inspire his country to their first-ever Test victory.

To the possible disbelief of the rest of the cricketing world, the top-ranked batsman in Test cricket for a period just after the turn of the millennium came from Zimbabwe. Over a thirteen-match stretch he scored 1,631 runs at an average of 108.73, propelling himself to the top of the ICC Test batting charts, taking over top spot from Sachin Tendulkar. For a nation still taking its first tentative steps in the international arena, he provided the stability for a country rocked by instability. His performances didn't just leave his peers in his wake, but the rest of the cricketing world too.

At Nagpur in 2000, he kept wicket for 155 overs as India posted 609/6 and didn't concede a single bye. When the inevitable follow-on was enforced, he struck an unbeaten 232 to save the game, which remains the highest Test score by any wicketkeeper.

Score	Player	Match	Venue	Year
232*	A. Flower	Zimbabwe v India	Nagpur	2000
230	K.C. Sangakkara	Sri Lanka v Pakistan	Lahore	2002
224	MS Dhoni	India v Australia	Chennai	2013
219*	Mushfiqur Rahim	Bangladesh v Zimbabwe	Mirpur	2018
210*	Taslim Arif	Pakistan v Australia	Faisalabad	1980

Ten months later, it was a case of déjà vu. South Africa were the visitors to Harare, and they made a bye-less 600/3. Flower then scored 142 out of Zimbabwe's first-innings 286, and 199 not out in the follow-on, in the process batting for longer than anyone else has in a Test that has ended in a defeat for his side.

Player	Minutes	Match	Venue	Year
A. Flower	879	Zimbabwe v South Africa	Harare	2001
M.H. Richardson	813	New Zealand v England	Lord's	2004
H. Sutcliffe	810	England v Australia	Melbourne	1925
D.M. Bravo	804	West Indies v Pakistan	Dubai (DSC)	2016
A. Flower	754	Zimbabwe v Sri Lanka	Harare	1999

That run couldn't last forever, and with the atmosphere at home uneasy due to increasing political tensions, he staged his 'black armband' protest with Henry Olonga in the 2003 World Cup fixture against Namibia. He was never to play international cricket again after that tournament but enjoyed several highly successful seasons for Essex before achieving even greater heights as England's coach.

Mark Boucher   **international career 1997–2012**

'As a player he was a man for the trenches. He had a way about him that he could dig deep down and play the percentages. It is rare to find that in a player and Boucher had that ability. As a person he always stood up for what he believed in, but he was also a great team man.' Pat Symcox

Even though Mark Boucher had been a permanent fixture in international cricket for fifteen years and had indicated that the 2012 tour of England might be his last, there was still a sense of deep shock when a freak eye injury put an end to his career before the First Test had been played.

In the modern era in which he found himself, there was more pressure than ever on wicketkeepers to have more than a solitary string to their bow. Boucher certainly didn't disappoint in that respect, frequently rescuing his side from choppy waters in Test cricket, or scripting phenomenal victories in the shorter form of the game.

He always seemed to be there at the key moments in South African cricket, taking four catches in the heartbreaking World Cup semi-final defeat in 1999. Four years later, he was on strike and turned down the single to midwicket, which sealed their elimination from their home tournament after another tie. It was he who hit the winning runs in the never-to-be-forgotten 872-run Johannesburg ODI in March 2006, and his calm, unbeaten 45 at Edgbaston in 2008 helped seal South Africa's first Test series victory in England for more than forty years.

Throughout his career he had the privilege of keeping wicket to some of the finest fast bowlers in the world – this was a time when South Africa produced Allan Donald, Shaun Pollock, Makhaya Ntini, Dale Steyn and Morne Morkel. Therefore, when his premature retirement came, it was not surprising that he had clocked up more dismissals behind the stumps in international cricket than anyone else.

Player	Matches	Dismissals	Catches	Stumpings
M.V. Boucher	**466**	**998**	**952**	**46**
A.C. Gilchrist	391	**905**	813	92
MS Dhoni	538	**829**	634	195
K.C. Sangakkara	464	**671**	532	139
I.A. Healy	87	**628**	560	68

Boucher may have ended up two short of a thousand, but he would be the first to point out that he did take one catch in the field – in an ODI at Port of Spain in 2010, moving him up to 999. And then there was his Test wicket: he removed Dwayne Bravo with his eighth ball in Test cricket at St John's in 2005, thereby making a total of 1,000 batsmen in whose dismissal he had a hand in.

With the bat, no matter what dire straits he might have found his team in, he was always positive, striding to the middle with purpose. He was the first to volunteer for nightwatchman duties and he carved his name into the record books as the first player to score two centuries in that role.

Score	Batsman	Match	Venue	Year
201*	J.N. Gillespie	Australia v Bangladesh	Chittagong	2006
125	**M.V. Boucher**	**South Africa v Zimbabwe**	**Harare**	**1999**
108	**M.V. Boucher**	**South Africa v England**	**Durban**	**1999**
105	A.L. Mann	Australia v India	Perth	1977
101*	S.M.H. Kirmani	India v Australia	Mumbai	1979
101	Nasim-ul-Ghani	Pakistan v England	Lord's	1962

Seven years post-retirement, he was appointed his country's national coach and given the opportunity to try to instil into a new South African team the kind of determination that made him such a relentless, competitive player for so many years.

Rodney Marsh   **international career 1970–84**

'Never one to cower meekly, always prepared to bite off more than most men could chew.' Paul Sheehan

For a man who was christened 'Iron Gloves' early in his career to sign off from Test cricket as the leading wicketkeeper the game had ever known must have taken supreme effort and dedication to his art. Ian Healy and Adam Gilchrist followed him and arguably achieved greater heights with the team, but to many, Marsh remains the greatest Australian keeper of all.

He and his brother Graham – later a professional golfer who racked up seventy tournament victories – played countless backyard matches, before diverging to follow their own sporting paths to success.

At the age of 8, Rodney was already keeping wicket in a local Under-16 team, but he considered batting to be his main strength. Indeed, it was on the back of his batting that he was able to progress through grade cricket and he made his first-class debut as a specialist number five batsman.

That debut came against the touring West Indians at the WACA in October 1968, and what a baptism of fire it was. The tourists boasted Wes Hall, Charlie Griffith and Garry Sobers in their team, and it was Griffith who dismissed Marsh in the first innings for a duck. He fared somewhat better second time around, striking 104, and his career was up and running.

He soon became the epitome of Australian cricket in the 1970s – competitive, hard, and the consummate team player, who was always capable of inspiring his colleagues to greater feats. He grew to embrace the Iron Gloves moniker, given as it was after he conceded 44 byes in the disappointing 1970/71 home Ashes series defeat. He was determined to lift the standard of his keeping and he did just that – acrobatically flinging himself about to stop Lillee and Thomson's thunderbolts.

The 1977 Centenary Test at Melbourne was memorable for many reasons, not least in that it provided the same result as the Test it commemorated – a 45-run victory for Australia. It was Marsh who lit it up, breaking Wally Grout's Australian record of 187 Test dismissals and then becoming the first of just four Australian wicketkeepers to score a Test century against England.

Score	Name	Venue	Year
110*	R.W. Marsh	Melbourne	1977
102*	I.A. Healy	Manchester	1993
134	I.A. Healy	Brisbane	1998
152	A.C. Gilchrist	Birmingham	2001
133	A.C. Gilchrist	Sydney	2003
102*	A.C. Gilchrist	Perth	2006
121	B.J. Haddin	Cardiff	2009
136	B.J. Haddin	Brisbane	2010
118	B.J. Haddin	Adelaide	2013

It could have come earlier. In just his fourth Test, he was 92 not out when Bill Lawry declared Australia's first innings closed at Melbourne in order to have an hour to bowl at England on the second evening. Rather than be disappointed at the missed opportunity, Marsh stated that he felt he had gained 40 runs as Lawry should have declared earlier!

Marsh played his last Test at Sydney in 1984 against Pakistan. In that match, Abdul Qadir became the ninety-fifth and final batsman to be dismissed c Marsh b Lillee – still a record to this day.

Keeper	Bowler	Matches	Catches
R.W. Marsh	D.K. Lillee	69	95
A.C. Gilchrist	G.D. McGrath	71	90
M.V. Boucher	M. Ntini	96	84
A.C. Gilchrist	B. Lee	65	81
M.V. Boucher	S.M. Pollock	88	79
B.J. Haddin	M.G. Johnson	52	71
P.J.L. Dujon	M.D. Marshall	68	71

He had his moments in ODI cricket too, hitting the winning run in the first match of its type ever played back in 1971. He also struck 26 from the first five deliveries of a Lance Cairns over at Adelaide in November 1980 before being dismissed from the final ball.

Post-retirement, he played a crucial role in the development of the Australian Cricket Academy, being influential in the early careers of Ricky Ponting, Glenn McGrath, Adam Gilchrist and Brett Lee. He then accepted the invitation to perform a similar role in England, helping to put the wheels in motion that culminated in the 2005 Ashes victory.

MS Dhoni   international career 2004–19

'If first appearances are important, Dhoni is a winner. Corporate India obviously thinks so. He has become an icon of modern India.' Greg Chappell

In late 2008, MS Dhoni went for a haircut. Not such an unusual occurrence, but it made front-page news in India. In fact, it was probably the most famous haircut since Elvis Presley had his locks shorn when he was called up into the army exactly fifty years earlier.

More a natural athlete than a natural wicketkeeper, his batting technique also had its flaws, but he was often able to turn it on just when it mattered most, specialising in hitting sixes to win games from improbable positions.

He first came to attention by striking 148 against India at Visakhapatnam in just his fifth ODI – having scored just 22 runs in total in his four previous innings. And soon after he hit an unbeaten 183 against Sri Lanka in October 2005, he was promoted to the Test side, his long flowing locks making him the poster boy in the Indian team.

Cricket hadn't had much of a history of successful wicketkeeper captains. Gerry Alexander had probably been the most effective, but he only led the West Indies in eighteen Tests over a two-year period. He also had the firepower of Walcott, Worrell, Weekes, Sobers, Hall and Griffith to call upon in his ranks. Dhoni changed that notion, and ended up combining the dual role of wicketkeeper and captain in more matches than anyone else in international cricket – and it isn't even close.

Captain	Team	Years	Matches
MS Dhoni	**Ind**	**2007–2018**	**332**
Sarfaraz Ahmed	Pak	2015–2019	**100**
Mushfiqur Rahim	Ban	2011–2017	**81**
K.C. Sangakkara	SL	2009–2012	**67**
A. Flower	Zim	1993–2000	**62**

His first appointment as captain came in the ICC World Twenty20 in South Africa in 2007. No one gave India much of a chance, but on a famous night in Johannesburg, Dhoni handed the ball to Joginder Sharma to close out the match against Pakistan. It paid off, as Misbah-ul-Haq's attempted flick over short fine leg ended up in the hands of Sreesanth to give India the title.

That victory led to untold riches for Dhoni as he became the most expensive signing in the inaugural Indian Premier League in 2008, sold to the Chennai Super Kings for $1.5m. Leading the team to three titles, he earned more money from the league than anyone else.

Player	Earnings (USD)
MS Dhoni	**$19.4m**
R.G. Sharma	**$18.5m**
V. Kohli	**$17.7m**
S.K. Raina	**$14.0m**
G. Gambhir	**$13.3m**
AB de Villiers	**$12.9m**
Yuvraj Singh	**$11.9m**
S.P. Narine	**$11.6m**
S.R. Watson	**$10.8m**
R.V. Uthappa	**$10.6m**

He led the Indian Test team to top spot in the ICC's Test rankings for the first time in November 2009, a position they held for eighteen months. However, his crowning glory came in the 2011 World Cup. With the host nation desperate to end a twenty-eight-year wait to repeat their upset 1983 triumph, he struck the trophy-winning six off Sri Lanka's Nuwan Kulasekara in the final in Mumbai to send a billion fans into rapture.

In 2013, he became the first captain to win all three major ICC events when India won the Champions Trophy in England, but he retired from Test cricket at the end of the following year. Fortunately for fans around the world, he had no intention of hanging up his coloured pads and carried on guiding a new generation of Indian youngsters keen to follow in his footsteps.

Les Ames   international career 1929–39

'Discreet and disarming destruction, with his conjuror's hands, was the wicketkeeping style of Les Ames. It contrasted with the swagger and glee of his batting, which yielded 102 centuries, most, if not all, those of an entertainer in a hurry.' Alan Hill

The 1930s must have been a hard time for bowlers. At the top of the tree were Bradman, Hammond and Headley, but the second rung of talent would have graced any other era in Test history. Sutcliffe, McCabe, Hendren, Paynter and Mitchell gave hours of batting entertainment to crowds throughout the world.

In the recent past we have been spoiled by wicketkeeper-batsmen. But rewind to the 1930s, and there was Les Ames, the first great wicketkeeper-batsman in Test history. Before Ames, there had only been two centuries by wicketkeepers in over fifty years of Test cricket. Ames scored eight all by himself and was a good enough batsman to have been selected for England on that basis alone.

He was advised to take up wicketkeeping in order to have another string to his bow and it was said that he made the art of keeping look easy, which is as high a compliment as can be paid.

His critics might point out that only one of his eight Test centuries came in his seventeen Ashes Tests, and it was overshadowed by Hedley Verity's fifteen wickets at Lord's in 1934. However, Ames gorged himself on the lesser international bowling attacks of the time. Most notably, his 123 runs before lunch in the 1935 Oval Test against South Africa remained a record until Ben Stokes beat it at Cape Town in 2016.

He made a habit of achieving the wicketkeeper's 'double' of 1,000 runs and 100 dismissals in a season – upping the ante in 1932 with 2,482 runs and 104 dismissals. The following year he broke the 3,000-run barrier and ended his career with 102 first-class centuries, of which fifty-seven were made when he was the specialist wicketkeeper, far more than anyone else in cricket history.

Player	100s
L.E.G. Ames	**57**
Kamran Akmal	**33**
A.C. Gilchrist	**29**
J.M. Parks	**27**
J.K. Silva	**26**

But above everything, he remained a man of Kent. His partnership with 'Tich' Freeman combined to dismiss more batsmen than any other combination in first-class history.

Keeper	Bowler	Matches	Catches	Stumpings	Dismissals
L.E.G. Ames	**A.P. Freeman**	**269**	**82**	**259**	**341**
F.H. Huish	C. Blythe	371	153	166	**319**
D. Hunter	W. Rhodes	326	141	164	**305**
H. Elliott	T.B. Mitchell	298	118	158	**276**
E.W. Pooley	J. Southerton	192	124	148	**272**

Ames was also a talented footballer, playing as an outside left for Clapton Orient before making five appearances for Gillingham in 1931/32, scoring a goal away against Bristol Rovers at Eastgate Stadium in the old Third Division South. However, that solitary goal came after the Gills had already conceded five goals in the first half in what ended up a 5-2 defeat.

After retirement, Ames spent fifteen years as secretary and manager of his beloved Kent side, which coincided with their successful years in the 1970s.

Godfrey Evans   international career 1946–59

'The word brilliant is the most shop-soiled in the language. But for Evans the word is semantically exact ... to Evans showmanship was natural; it was his bravura way of doing things.' A.A. Thomson

It was said of some keepers that they were hardly noticed, but that could never have been levelled at Godfrey Evans. He loved the theatrical nature of his profession, never more in evidence than when pulling off another leg-side stumping. As Les Ames neared the twilight of his Kent career, Evans saw these theatricals as a way of drawing attention to the fact that he should be the designated successor.

He was not a Man of Kent by birth, but his family moved there when he was less than a year old, and he attended Kent College, where he excelled at boxing, as well as captaining the school side at cricket, football and hockey. In those days he seldom kept wicket, as that was a position seen as perfect to hide a less mobile fielder.

He joined the Kent staff and had made just five first-class appearances before the Second World War put an end to his professional cricket career for seven long years. When hostilities ended, he soon established himself as England's number one choice, a position he was not to relinquish until the end of the following decade.

His Test debut came in a rain-ruined match against India at The Oval in August 1946. On a difficult pitch, India scored 331 the only time they batted and Evans let through just one bye. However, that solitary bye off Jim Langridge's slow left-arm spin would be a cause of annoyance to him until his dying day.

With the bat he lit up the record books in ways that ranged from the sublime to the ridiculous. As Denis Compton attempted to reach his second century of the match at Adelaide in 1947, Evans spent ninety-seven minutes before scoring his first run, which remained a record for more than half a century.

Minutes	Player	Match	Venue	Year
103	S.C.J. Broad	England v New Zealand	Auckland	2013
101	G.I. Allott	New Zealand v South Africa	Auckland	1999
97	**T.G. Evans**	**England v Australia**	**Adelaide**	**1947**

It was also at Adelaide in 1955 that Evans struck the boundary, which ensured the retention of the Ashes on Len Hutton's triumphant tour.

Against India at Lord's in 1952, he joined Tom Graveney at the start of the third day. Nursing a sore head from the excesses of the night before, he attacked from the start and narrowly missed out scoring a century before lunch. He ended 98 not out at the break when umpire Frank Chester called 'time' after Vijay Hazare spent an age rearranging his field. To this day, only two players have scored more runs before lunch in a Lord's Test.

Player	Match	Year	Runs
W. Bardsley (164)	Australia v South Africa	1912	118
J.B. Hobbs (211)	England v South Africa	1924	102
T.G. Evans (104)	**England v India**	**1952**	**98**

At Leeds in 1966, he caught Collie Smith from the bowling of Don Smith to become the first wicketkeeper to make 200 dismissals in Test cricket. He carried on for another three years, before ending his career as the most-capped Test player of all time, with ninety-one appearances – a remarkable achievement for a wicketkeeper. At the time, no one else had spent more than Bert Oldfield's fifty-four Tests behind the stumps.

After retirement he became a publican, famously sporting lambchop sideburns, which became his trademark later in life. He made a surprise comeback to the Kent side in 1967 at the age of 46, when Alan Knott was away with England, keeping immaculately, by all accounts!

He also found work as a cricket expert for Ladbrokes, as he was valued as a shrewd assessor of the state of play. However, he got one catastrophically wrong! It was he who suggested the famous odds of 500/1 on an England victory at Headingley in 1981, which ended up costing his employers £21,000 – admittedly, most of it to Dennis Lillee and Rodney Marsh.

Chapter 5

Fast Bowlers

Dennis Lillee   international career 1971–84

'There's no batsman on earth who goes out to face Dennis Lillee and Jeff Thomson with a smile on his face.' Clive Lloyd

Growing up, one of the magical numbers in cricket was 355. That marked the record for the most wickets in Test cricket, and the owner of that record was Dennis Lillee. Currently that number is outside the top twenty, but there is little doubt that Dennis Lillee was one of the finest bowlers of all time.

Born in Subiaco, an early inspiration was his teacher at Belmay Primary School, Ken Waters, who taught him football, athletics and cricket as well as instilling in him a fierce determination to win. He subsequently joined Perth Cricket Club when he was 15, taking 1-23 against Fremantle in his first match. It wasn't long before he progressed through the ranks and made a first-class debut for Western Australia in October 1969.

In just his fifth first-class match he hit the headlines by cutting a swathe through the South Australian batting to finish with figures of 7-36 at the WACA. It was a harsh jolt back to reality the following year when he bowled eighteen fruitless overs as Barry Richards scored 325 in a day, but with Australia one down in the Ashes series, he was selected to make a Test debut against England at Adelaide in January 1971.

Australia had been waiting for a fast-bowling successor to Alan Davidson for a decade, and whereas they had Graham McKenzie and Neil Hawke, no one really struck fear into opposition batsmen's hearts. Lillee didn't disappoint – tearing in with his customary shirt unbuttoned and gold chain jangling – to take 5-84 in England's first innings.

South Africa's proposed tour of Australia in 1971 was cancelled, and so a series against a 'Rest of the World' XI took place instead. On his home ground at Perth he took 8-29 as the star-studded World team – featuring Sunil Gavaskar, Clive Lloyd, Garry Sobers and Tony Greig – were bowled out for just 59. At one stage, he took six wickets for no runs in fifteen deliveries.

He started the 1972 Ashes series with 6-66 in England's second innings at Old Trafford and finished with ten wickets in the Oval Test, to total thirty-one wickets in all, which ended up being somewhat overshadowed by Bob Massie's sixteen wickets at Lord's.

Something had to give, and that something was his back as he fractured his lower vertebrae in three places in 1973. The Australian Cricket Board refused to pay for his treatment so Lillee sought out his old PE teacher at Belmont High School, Frank Pyke, who designed an extensive rehabilitation programme that Lillee followed religiously.

Against all the odds, he came back after eighteen months with a remodelled action but managed to retain his hostility, as England discovered in the 1974/75 series when he and Jeff Thomson laid waste to the tourists' batting. The following summer, his twenty-seven wickets in Australia's 5-1 trouncing of the West Indies in 1975/76 led Clive Lloyd to pursue the same fast-bowling formula for the next two decades.

Controversy was never too far away. He produced an aluminium bat at Perth in 1979, which he subsequently flung away, and he had to be separated from Javed Miandad by umpire Tony Crafter after a contretemps a couple of years later. He also missed a couple of years' Test cricket to play World Series Cricket for Kerry Packer, in which he took more wickets in the Supertests than anyone else.

Player	Team	Matches	Wickets	Avge
D.K. Lillee	**Aus**	14	67	26.87
A.M.E. Roberts	WI	13	50	24.14
R.J. Bright	Aus	15	42	29.71
M.A. Holding	WI	9	35	23.09
J. Garner	WI	7	35	24.77

Lillee, Greg Chappell and Rod Marsh all said farewell to Test cricket after the Sydney Test with Pakistan in 1984. As Lillee strode from the arena for the final time, he was the leading wicket-taker in Test cricket with that magical number that was even more beautifully the same number of dismissals effected by Marsh behind the stumps.

Player	Team	Wickets
D.K. Lillee	**Aus**	355
L.R. Gibbs	WI	309
F.S. Trueman	Eng	307
R.G.D. Willis	Eng	305
D.L. Underwood	Eng	297

Malcolm Marshall   international career 1978–92

'Malcolm played cricket on a different level. He basically had the ability to do what he wanted with the ball and when he wanted to do it, and what speed he wanted to do it.' Graeme Fowler

The all-conquering West Indian teams of the 1970s and 1980s boasted a host of fast bowlers. Most fitted a certain mould – tall and menacing. But the one among them who was acknowledged to be the greatest was of average height and build. What he lacked in build he made up for in speed of run-up and release, and was a master of the swinging ball. He was also a better batsman than all the rest, coming closest to being a world-class all-rounder.

Born in Barbados in 1958, just a couple of months after Garry Sobers had broken the Test individual score record, it was no surprise that the young Malcolm Marshall grew up idolising the all-rounder. He lost his father when he was only a year old, so learned his cricket from his grandfather, and didn't leave the island until he was selected for his first cricket tour.

Having played just one first-class match, in which he took 6-77 against Jamaica, he was picked to tour India in 1978/79, with the West Indies short of fast-bowling talent due to World Series cricket. Marshall played three Tests on that tour and took only three wickets, but showed enough promise to be taken on by Hampshire as a successor to Andy Roberts. In 1980, he was instrumental in an English collapse of seven wickets for just 24 runs at Manchester. Despite that, it would be another two years until he made himself a regular in the international side.

He spent his time honing his skill on English pitches. Having taken sixty-six first-class wickets in 1980 and sixty-eight the following year, his performance in 1982 was staggering as he took 134 wickets – exactly the sum of his two previous years. No one has bettered that tally in English first-class cricket since the fixtures were dramatically reduced in 1969.

Player	Year	Matches	Wickets	Avge
M.D. Marshall	**1982**	**22**	**134**	**15.73**
L.R. Gibbs	1971	26	**131**	18.89
F.D. Stephenson	1988	22	**125**	18.31
R.D. Jackman	1980	23	**121**	15.40
A.M.E. Roberts	1974	21	**119**	13.62

In 1983, he established himself in the West Indies team, taking twenty-one wickets in the series against India, and bowling superbly in the World Cup. Thirty-three more wickets followed as the West Indies exerted some manner of revenge over the Indians for their World Cup final defeat.

The following year in England, he ended Andy Lloyd's Test career after half an hour with a blow to the helmet but broke his thumb at Headingley trying to stop a stroke from Chris Broad. Unperturbed, he came in to bat last and successfully shepherded Larry Gomes to a century before taking seven wickets for 53 with the lower part of his left arm in plaster.

Having graduated to a West Indian side alongside Roberts, Holding and Garner, he became the acknowledged leader of the pack in the early years of Ambrose, Patterson and Walsh. He set the tone for the 1985/86 season by breaking Mike Gatting's nose with a bouncer and took twenty-seven wickets in that 5-0 series whitewash, but he was arguably never better than in the 1988 'summer of four captains' in England.

He took thirty-five wickets in that series, including a career-best 7-22 at Manchester, and had a farewell tour of England three years later when he ended his career with the best bowling average of any Test bowler with at least 200 wickets.

Player	Team	Wickets	Avge
M.D. Marshall	**WI**	**376**	**20.94**
J. Garner	WI	259	**20.97**
C.E.L. Ambrose	WI	405	**20.99**
F.S. Trueman	Eng	307	**21.57**
G.D. McGrath	Aus	563	**21.64**

His 376 Test wickets were a West Indian record until Courtney Walsh went past it years later. As was the case with Victor Trumper almost a century earlier, the whole cricket world mourned when he succumbed to cancer at the tragically early age of 41.

Wasim Akram   international career 1984–2003

'In Akram's hands a ball does not so much talk as sing. With a flick of the wrist and an arm that flashes past his ears like a thought through a child's brain he pushes the ball across the batsmen and makes it dip back wickedly late.' Peter Roebuck

By the age of 12, Wasim Akram was opening both batting and bowling for the Cathedral School in Lahore, and three years later he was the captain. Growing up, he spent all his spare time playing competitive games of cricket, which dominated the evenings in the Lahore streets. His performances in these matches soon won him a place to the Pakistan Board's talent camp at the age of 18.

He soon progressed to the Under-19 set-up, where one day Javed Miandad turned up for a net. He was so impressed with Akram's command of pace and swing that he immediately included him in the squad for the BCCP Patron's XI to face the touring New Zealanders at Rawalpindi. He took 7-50 in the first innings and won himself an ODI debut a fortnight later. His Test debut came in early 1985 and he was immediately into the swing of the longer format, taking ten wickets in only his second Test.

Cricket had seen left-arm fast bowlers before, but they were few and far between. The best had probably been Alan Davidson, with most of the others operating at very much below top speed. Wasim Akram soared past the rest on his way to becoming the only left-arm fast bowler to take 400 Test wickets and the leading wicket-taker in international cricket by any left-hander.

Player	Team	Matches	Wickets	Avge
Wasim Akram	**Pak**	**460**	**916**	**23.57**
W.P.U.J.C. Vaas	SL	439	**761**	28.44
D.L. Vettori	NZ	442	**705**	32.42
Z. Khan	Ind	309	**610**	31.14
M.G. Johnson	Aus	256	**590**	26.65

In his sixth ODI he faced the West Indies at Melbourne in the Benson & Hedges World Championship of Cricket. Pakistan won easily by seven wickets in what was Clive Lloyd's last international appearance. That farewell enabled 143 years of international cricket to be linked by just eight players.

George Ulyett played in the first Test in 1877, and then...

in 1890 played against Syd Gregory, who...

from 1899–1912 played against Wilfred Rhodes, who...

in 1930 played against George Headley, who...

in 1954 played against Tom Graveney, who...

in 1968 and 1969 played against Clive Lloyd, who...

in 1985 played against Wasim Akram, who...

in 2003 played against James Anderson, who was still playing international cricket in 2020.

On Imran Khan's recommendation, Akram spent the summer of 1986 playing for Burnopfield – Colin Milburn's old club – in the Durham League. He was then ready for the full tour of England with Pakistan the following summer, and on the first day he signed a six-year contract with Lancashire.

Pakistan won the Test series in England 1-0 and Akram became a legend at Lancashire. He scored a century in his second first-class match and helped them win both one-day cups in 1990, taking the crucial wicket of Graeme Hick in the Benson & Hedges final at Lord's. He would end up taking 374 first-class and 260 List A wickets for the county.

He debuted in the 1980s when fast bowling was more about intimidation than trying to bowl the opposition batsmen out. A generation of batsmen had bobbed, swayed and ducked out of the way. Akram – later with his teammate Waqar – changed all that by bowling quickly and accurately at the stumps, and often hitting them or the poor unsuspecting batsman's legs, which just so happened to be in the way.

He had a great role model in Imran Khan and he also learned tricks from Malcolm Marshall, Richard Hadlee and Franklyn Stephenson, among others. He also possessed the key left-arm skill of bringing the ball back into the batsman. His two deliveries to Allan Lamb and Chris Lewis swung the 1992 World Cup final decisively in Pakistan's direction and earned him the Player of the Match award.

He was a natural ball-striker too but under-achieved in that facet of the game, averaging a mere 22.64 over the course of his Test career. There were a few highlights though – a crucial unbeaten 45 shepherded his side to a Test victory at Lord's in 1992, and an unbeaten 257 against Zimbabwe in 1996, which included the most sixes in a Test innings.

Player	Runs	6s	Match	Venue	Year
Wasim Akram	**257***	**12**	**Pakistan v Zimbabwe**	**Sheikhupura**	**1996**
N.J. Astle	222	11	New Zealand v England	Christchurch	2002
M.L. Hayden	380	11	Australia v Zimbabwe	Perth	2003
B.B. McCullum	202	11	New Zealand v Pakistan	Sharjah	2014
B.B. McCullum	195	11	New Zealand v Sri Lanka	Christchurch	2014
B.A. Stokes	258	11	England v South Africa	Cape Town	2016

Sydney Barnes   international career 1901–14

'Like all the best bowling craftsmen he hated batsmen and believed that every ball delivered should be their last.' Bernard Hollowood

Born in Smethwick in Staffordshire, Barnes made four unremarkable appearances for Warwickshire from 1894 to 1896, but in need of money he signed for Rishton in the Lancashire League, with whom he played for five seasons. In 1898, they won the league and Barnes was the league's leading wicket-taker, and having moved to Burnley in 1900, he helped them to the title the following year.

Barnes' haul of wickets in the league summer of 1901 attracted the attention of England captain Archie MacLaren ahead of their forthcoming tour to Australia. MacLaren invited Barnes to Old Trafford to see how this young bowler had gained such a reputation. After hitting MacLaren on the thigh and gloves, he was told: 'You're coming to Australia with me.' His international career started thanks to a net session.

He was an uncoached, self-made bowler, whose high upright action enabled him to obtain surprising lift from the pitch. He could move the ball both ways in the air and was proficient with both off and leg breaks delivered at a brisk medium pace. It all added up to a bowler who could perform superbly not just in England, but on the matting wickets in South Africa and the hard pitches in Australia. His final asset was his stamina, keeping on at the batsman until he found success, which invariably came.

On his Test debut at Sydney, he took 5-65 and 1-74, and then took thirteen wickets in the Second Test at Melbourne. His reputation was made. On returning from the tour he joined Lancashire and took 131 first-class wickets in 1903 but fell out with the club over winter employment. From then onwards he was to only play league cricket.

His reputation for being a difficult character led to his absence from the England team for five years, but when he finally returned, his Test performances were remarkable. He took twenty-four and thirty-four wickets in the 1907/08 and 1911/12 Ashes series respectively, and thirty-nine more in six Tests in the 1912 Triangular series with Australia and South Africa. He saved his best for last though, when, at the age of 40, he was unplayable on the matting wickets on England's 1913/14 tour of South Africa.

Barnes started with ten wickets at Durban, then, in the Second Test at Johannesburg, he took seventeen wickets for 159 – a record match haul that stood until Jim Laker beat it in 1956. Eight wickets followed at the same venue before he took seven wickets in each innings of what was to be his final Test back at Durban. He finished the series with forty-nine wickets, which remains a record to this day.

Player	Team	Against	Season	Matches	Wickets
S.F. Barnes	**Eng**	**SA**	**1913/14**	**4**	**49**
J.C. Laker	Eng	Aus	1956	5	46
C.V. Grimmett	Aus	SA	1935/36	5	44
T.M. Alderman	Aus	Eng	1981	6	42
R.M. Hogg	Aus	Eng	1978/79	6	41
T.M. Alderman	Aus	Eng	1989	6	41

He also ended his career with retrospectively the highest ICC Test bowling rating of any bowler in history.

Player	Team	Date	Points
S.F. Barnes	**Eng**	**Feb 1914**	**932**
G.A. Lohmann	Eng	Mar 1896	931
Imran Khan	Pak	Jan 1983	922
M. Muralitharan	SL	Jul 2007	920
G.D. McGrath	Aus	Aug 2001	914
P.J. Cummins	Aus	Aug 2019	914

Less than four months later, the world was at war and there was no more Test cricket for seven years, therefore ending Barnes' career with a record 189 wickets in just twenty-seven Tests — exactly seven wickets per match. As he was too old for military service, he joined Saltaire Cricket Club, where he played for eight seasons, helping them to three Bradford League championships.

He was asked to tour Australia again aged 47, but declined when his family were not allowed to join him on the trip. However, he ploughed on in the leagues until well into his sixties, ending his club career with 4,069 wickets and a staggering total of 6,229 in all forms of the game — at an average of 8.33.

Glenn McGrath   **international career 1993–2007**

'England have no McGrathish bowlers, there are hardly any McGrathish bowlers, except for McGrath.' Stuart Law

Glenn McGrath's Test career began relatively slowly, with just nineteen wickets coming in his first eight Tests, at an average of 43.68. However, the retirement of Craig McDermott spurred him on and for more than a decade he caused havoc for batsmen all over the world with his accuracy and ability to obtain bounce from a good length.

Born in Dubbo, he went to school in nearby Narromine, where he learned to play cricket. However, there was only one turf wicket available, with concrete more frequently used. At the age of 17 he had improved enough to be selected for the New South Wales Country Cup, and a chance meeting with Doug Walters changed his life.

On Walters' recommendation, two years later he moved to Sydney and started playing grade cricket for Sutherland, but he still had a long journey ahead. He spent four years working odd jobs and living in a caravan while playing cricket at the weekends, before he made his first-class debut for New South Wales in January 1993, just short of his twenty-third birthday. He took 5-79 in 29.1 overs in the first innings, and by the end of the year he was in the Test team.

On paper it appeared to be a very simple method but his easy approach to the wicket and high-arm, rhythmical, economical action prevented the serious injuries that derailed many of his fast-bowling contemporaries. That longevity enabled him to end his career with 563 Test wickets – more than any other seam bowler in the history of the game at the time of his retirement. It wasn't just the tally of wickets though, but the way he got people out, as Michael Atherton and Brian Lara would testify. Lara averaged more than 100 against the combined wiles of Muralitharan and Warne, but just 27 against McGrath.

By the time Australia toured the West Indies in 1995 to win their seminal series and take over the undisputed crown as the number one Test team, McGrath was leading their attack. He was instrumental in the 1997 Ashes triumph, taking 8-38 at Lord's and 7-76 at The Oval, which demonstrated his love for the big occasion. To this day, no overseas bowler has taken more wickets at Lord's.

Player	Matches	Wickets	Avge
G.D. McGrath	**3**	**26**	**11.50**
R.J. Hadlee	4	26	21.26
M.D. Marshall	3	20	17.00
C.A. Walsh	4	20	22.95
C.T.B. Turner	3	19	14.63
S.K. Warne	4	19	19.57

McGrath's 300th Test wicket was Brian Lara in the middle of a hat-trick at Perth, and his 500th came at Lord's in 2005 when he delivered a spell of five wickets for 2 runs to help bowl Australia to yet another victory at Headquarters. However, that series ended in a 2-1 defeat, with the two losses coming in Tests McGrath missed – at Edgbaston when he injured his ankle after stepping on a ball in training, and at Trent Bridge when he was out with an elbow problem.

He finally retired from Test cricket after the 5-0 triumph in 2006/07 avenged the previous defeat, and later in 2007 won his third World Cup winner's medal. His bowling figures of 7-15 against Namibia in the 2003 competition remains a tournament record.

Bowling	Player	Match	Venue	Year
7-15	**G.D. McGrath**	**Australia v Namibia**	**Potchefstroom**	**2003**
7-20	A.J. Bichel	Australia v England	Port Elizabeth	2003
7-33	T.G. Southee	New Zealand v England	Wellington – W	2015
7-51	W.W. Davis	West Indies v Australia	Leeds	1983
6-14	G.J. Gilmour	Australia v England	Leeds	1975

Waqar Younis   international career 1989–2003

'You don't need a helmet facing Waqar so much as a steel toe-cap.' Simon Hughes

Not many cricketers can claim that a new word was invented for them, but in the early 1990s, a new verb was invented. To be 'Waqared' was to have been cleaned up – either lbw or bowled by a fast in-swinging yorker from the Pakistani speedster.

He was born in Burewala in the Vehari area of the Punjab, but was raised in Sharjah, where his father was a contract worker. He returned to Pakistan in his teens but played in relative obscurity until he was spotted while bowling in a televised local game by a convalescing Imran Khan from his bed. Imran saw something in the youngster he liked and took him under his wing. After just twelve first-class matches, Younis made his Test debut against India at Karachi in November 1989 – the same match in which Sachin Tendulkar debuted.

He took four wickets in the first innings – including that of Tendulkar dismissed bowled. It was also the start of his new-ball partnership with Wasim Akram, with whom he caused havoc against New Zealand in late 1990 with twenty-nine wickets in just three matches. His fast, long run-up combined with both pace and late swing had started to be an irresistible combination that spelled doom to batsmen around the world. That winter he became the first – and, so far, only – bowler to take three successive five-wicket hauls in ODI cricket.

5wl	Player	Start	End	Figures
3	Waqar Younis	04/11/1990	09/11/1990	5-11 v NZ, 5-16 v NZ, 5-52 v WI
2	12 bowlers			

He signed for Surrey on the back of a solitary net, and had a memorable 1991 season, taking 113 wickets at just 14.65 each. England found him and Wasim Akram too hot to handle the following year as Pakistan won the Test series 2-1. A common theme was the reverse swing the bowlers managed to find, which frequently saw wickets tumbling after England had made solid starts.

After thirty-one Tests he had racked up an incredible 180 wickets at an average of 18.78, with only Sydney Barnes having taken fewer Tests to claim the same number of wickets. His technique marked a change in the modus operandi of pace bowlers. Whereas they had concentrated on short-pitched bowling in the past, now they looked to bowl fast and full.

Waqar was unfortunate when it came to World Cups. He missed the victorious 1992 campaign with a back injury, and Ajay Jadeja found him much to his liking in the 1996 quarter-final. Pakistan reached the final in 1999 but imploded against Australia at Lord's, and finally, as captain in 2003, the team failed to progress beyond the group stage. Nevertheless, he boasted thirteen five-wicket hauls in all ODI cricket – a record that still stands.

Player	Team	5wl
Waqar Younis	**Pak**	**13**
M. Muralitharan	SL	10
B. Lee	Aus	9
Shahid Afridi	Pak	9
S.L. Malinga	SL	8

He was also an accomplished enough batsman to score more than a thousand Test runs – the first to achieve the feat without a 50 to his name.

As seemed to be the case with many greats of the game, controversy was never too far away and there was constant suspicion of the nature of reverse swing. Whatever the conclusions though, there is no denying that he was pretty much the best exponent of the art.

Fred Trueman   **international career 1952–65**

'Generally speaking he was a liked person. You have to remember that most great cricketers are basically selfish, they look after number one. Fred wanted to bowl when he wanted to bowl and at the end he wanted to bowl.' Peter Parfitt

In his own words: 't'Finest Bloody Fast Bowler that Ever Drew Breath', and who is to disagree? Fred Trueman was the son of a miner who first played cricket at Maltby Hall School, where he was encouraged to become a fast bowler. He left school at 14 to work in a factory and started playing for Roche Abbey CC, but after he took twenty-five wickets for 37 runs in his first four matches, it was evident that he should be playing at a higher level, so he moved to Sheffield United in the Sheffield League. In the meantime, he lost his job as a bricklayer after telling the foreman to 'bugger off'. It wasn't the only time his mouth would get him into trouble.

Further successes brought an invitation to play for Yorkshire Boys under the tutelage of Bill Bowes and Arthur Mitchell, and he made his full Yorkshire debut in 1949 at the age of just 18. It only took him two years to fuse the combination of speed and control, and he took ninety wickets in 1951 at a cost of just 20.57 apiece.

While still on National Service in 1952, he burst onto the international scene on his home ground at Leeds, when he reduced India to 0 for four in their second innings. The following month, he took 8-31 against them at Manchester and ended his first Test series with twenty-nine wickets at 13.31 each.

He quickly became a hero – he was a genuine box office draw, combining searing pace with humour and often flying foul of the authorities. It all added up to a magical mix that dominated English cricket for more than a decade. He wasn't picked until the final Test of the triumphant 1953 Ashes series, and by the start of the 1957 season, he had played just seven Tests since his first series.

By then, though, he was a complete fast bowler. His natural outswing claimed many wickets, but he could also swing the ball in and possessed a lethal bouncer, yorker and a slower ball. His partnership with Brian Statham now became a permanent part of the England set-up and he went from strength to strength.

He took twenty-two wickets in the 1957 series with the West Indies and after the unhappy 1958/59 tour of Australia, he found the Indians again to his liking and took twenty-four cheap wickets the following summer. That was the first of seven successive full-length Test series in which he took at least twenty wickets, culminating with thirty-four in the summer of 1963, which remains a record for England against the West Indies in a single series.

Player	Season	Matches	Wickets	Avge
F.S. Trueman	**1963**	**5**	**34**	**17.47**
A.R.C. Fraser	1997/98	6	**27**	18.22
J.A. Snow	1967/68	4	**27**	18.66
D.G. Cork	1995	5	**26**	25.42
D. Gough	2000	5	**25**	21.20

There was time for a final hurrah the following year, when another perfect outswinger claimed Australia's Neil Hawke as his 300th Test wicket – the first bowler to get there, and the only one for more than a decade.

Player	Team	Year
F.S. Trueman	**England**	**1964**
L.R. Gibbs	West Indies	**1975**
D.K. Lillee	Australia	**1981**
R.G.D. Willis	England	**1983**
I.T. Botham	England	**1984**

Even though he played sixty-seven Tests in his career, he missed a further fifty-three due to injury or varying disputes with selectors. He claimed that four-letter words cost him another hundred Test wickets. At Leeds in 1961, he conjured up a spell of five wickets for no runs in twenty-four balls, having slept the previous night in his car in a car park.

But Trueman was more than just an exceptional fast bowler. He was a superb fielder and hard-hitting lower-order batsman of some talent. Later in life he was a forthright commentator, regaling listeners with anecdotes that were toned down for a family audience.

Richard Hadlee   international career 1973–90

'There has been no greater fascination in modern cricket than watching an over from Richard Hadlee when there was some response from the pitch or some help in the atmosphere.' Don Mosey

One of five sons of Walter Hadlee, who had captained New Zealand in eight Tests, Richard Hadlee graduated to not only become his country's greatest player but, on the death of Sir Edmund Hillary in 2008, a candidate for the accolade of 'Greatest Living New Zealander'.

By the time he left Christchurch Boys' High School, his brothers were opening the bowling for the Old Boys club, but Richard was keen to bowl with the new ball. So he joined Lancaster Park and in January 1972 made his debut for Canterbury. It didn't take him long to make his mark, as he took a hat-trick against Central Districts in just his third match.

His Test debut came the following year against Pakistan at the Basin Reserve, when he saw his first ball hit for four by Sadiq Mohammad. He took just two wickets in the match but showed some promise with the bat as he struck 46 from just forty-three deliveries. It wasn't enough though, and he was dropped for the remaining two matches of the series for his brother Dayle.

That set the scene for the next few years of his Test career – fleeting appearances, but just as often out of the team as in it. His first major success came against India at Wellington in February 1976, when he took 7-23 to bowl New Zealand to a series-levelling victory. From then on, he was not only a permanent fixture in the team, but virtually all of New Zealand's Test victories had his stamp on them.

When England toured in early 1978, he took 6-26 as England were demolished for just 64 at Wellington, which prompted a contract with Nottinghamshire that summer as they were looking for a replacement for Clive Rice, who had signed with Kerry Packer's World Series Cricket. He took seventy-five wickets at just 16.53 apiece, which proved to be the start of a decade-long love affair with the Trent Bridge side.

He developed a short run-up as he took 105 championship wickets in 1981, and three years later performed the 'double' – the first of only two occasions it has been achieved since the reduction in the number of first-class matches in 1969.

Player	Season	Matches	Runs	Wickets
R.J. Hadlee	**1984**	**24**	**1,179**	**117**
F.D. Stephenson	1988	22	1,018	125

His international career continued to go from strength to strength. His eleven wickets were instrumental in New Zealand's victory at Dunedin in 1980, which led to the only series defeat for the West Indies in the best part of two decades. He also helped New Zealand to a 2-1 series win in Australia in 1985, taking fifteen wickets at Brisbane, which included a national record 9-52 in the first innings, in which he caught the tenth batsman off Vaughan Brown.

Bowling	Player	Against	Venue	Year
9-52	**R.J. Hadlee**	**Australia**	**Brisbane**	**1985**
7-23	**R.J. Hadlee**	**India**	**Wellington**	**1975**
7-27	C.L. Cairns	West Indies	Hamilton	1999
7-39	N. Wagner	West Indies	Wellington	2017
7-52	C. Pringle	Pakistan	Faisalabad	1990

He followed up with seven wickets at Sydney and eleven at Perth. The Kiwis then also won the home series with their Trans-Tasman rivals 1-0, which included his 300th Test wicket.

His side-on position at delivery helped his natural outswing, and he subsequently added an inswinger and off-cutter to his armoury. Whereas his bowling was scientific in its approach, his batting was more one-dimensional and not quite up to the standards of the other 'big four' all-rounders of the 1980s. It was still good enough to give him two Test centuries.

Knighted during his final Test series, Hadlee signed off by dismissing Devon Malcolm with his final delivery – an apt way to finish a glittering Test career. He transformed New Zealand from the amateur era into a world-class side that could compete with the very best.

Dale Steyn   international career 2004–

'He likes fishing, horror movies, all the gory stuff, you know. I think it comes out in his bowling sometimes.' Graeme Smith

Cricketing history is littered with fast bowlers making batsmen hop, sway and duck their way out of trouble. After the heights of the time before the turn of the millennium, the 2000s and 2010s were a lean time in terms of out-and-out pace bowling. However, over that time one man stood head and shoulders above the others, and that man was Dale Steyn – bulging eyes, throbbing veins and all.

He grew up in Phalaborwa, in South Africa's rural north-east, on the border of the Kruger National Park, and spent most of his childhood obsessed with skateboarding and rock music. His school had a prouder rugby history and so he was never surrounded by the most competitive of the nation's cricketing schoolboys.

A first-class debut for Northerns came his way when he had just turned 20 – the same match in which AB de Villiers played his initial first-class match. Incredibly, fourteen months later, the two men were making another debut together – this time in Test cricket against England at Port Elizabeth. Steyn failed to impress in his three matches in the series, with his eight wickets costing 52 runs each, and he also bowled thirty-four no-balls, which led to his being dropped.

A short spell in England with Essex in 2005 was similarly fruitless but he worked hard on his craft and performed much better in the subsequent South African domestic season, when he took eight wickets in the SuperSport Series final for Titans against Dolphins at Kingsmead. That performance earned him a recall to international colours for the home series with New Zealand, and he never looked back.

After his slowish start, taking thirteen matches to take his first fifty Test wickets, his next fifty took just seven more. In 2008, he was named the ICC Test Cricketer of the Year after playing a major part as South Africa won a Test series in England for the first time since their readmission. His batting made headlines later in the year when he scored 76 to accompany his ten wickets in the Boxing Day Test at Melbourne to help his side clinch the series.

He continued to rack up the wickets, flying past 300 just five years later, before becoming the second South African to reach the 400 landmark in 2015 and eventually ending his career as his country's greatest Test wicket-taker of all time.

Player	Matches	**Wickets**	Avge
D.W. Steyn	93	**439**	**22.95**
S.M. Pollock	108	**421**	23.11
M. Ntini	101	**390**	28.82
A.A. Donald	72	**330**	22.25
M. Morkel	86	**309**	27.66

His main weapon was the outswinger but he also had a vicious bouncer, which was deceptively quick and seemed to follow the batsman. He also mastered reverse swing, which was never better displayed than at Nagpur in 2010, when he took 7-51 to lead South Africa to a memorable victory. Perhaps the greatest tribute to him is the fact that in Asia – so often the graveyard of fast bowling – he flourished, taking ninety-two wickets at just 24.11 apiece in his twenty-two Tests.

His luck with injuries ran out in 2013 when he suffered a groin strain in the Champions Trophy, a side strain later that year and a rib fracture in early 2014, a year in which he also had three hamstring strains. However, by then he had created a fantastic legacy and he returned to somewhere near his best form as New Zealand were defeated in 2016. By the time he retired from the longest form of the game he had spent more matches (265) ranked the top bowler than anyone else, and he had the best strike rate of anyone taking at least 200 wickets.

Player	Team	Wickets	**Strike Rate**
D.W. Steyn	**SA**	439	**42.39**
Waqar Younis	Pak	373	**43.50**
M.D. Marshall	WI	376	**46.77**
A.A. Donald	SA	330	**47.03**
M.A. Starc	Aus	244	**48.17**

Andy Roberts   **international career 1974–83**

'Cerebral, calculating, the Godfather of the modern West Indian pacemen.' Mike
Selvey

Andy Roberts' start was innocent enough – the son of a fisherman from Urlings
Village in Antigua, part of a family of fourteen. He grew up playing games with
his friends among the cornfields but didn't participate in a proper game of cricket
until he left school at the age of 16. However, his rise was swift and the following
year he debuted for St John's, and just a year later for the Leeward Islands in
first-class cricket.

A member of the Volunteers' Cricket Committee on the island took note and
wrote to Hampshire, suggesting the county had a look at the young speedster. As
a result, he was sent to Alf Gover's indoor school in Wandsworth, alongside Viv
Richards. Hampshire's captain, Richard Gilliat, visited the nets, liked what he saw
and invited him for a trial in 1973.

Before he could have that trial, a serious knee injury threatened to derail his
career, but he recovered in time to take forty wickets for Hampshire's Second XI.
It was enough to earn him a full-time deal for 1974, and he made a huge impact
on the county game by taking 119 wickets at an average of just 13.62 in first-class
cricket, the least expensive haul of at least a hundred wickets in a season since
the first-class fixtures were reduced in 1969.

Player	Year	Matches	Wickets	Avge
A.M.E. Roberts	**1974**	**21**	**119**	**13.62**
R.J. Hadlee	1984	24	117	**14.05**
D.L. Underwood	1978	22	110	**14.49**
Waqar Younis	1991	18	113	**14.65**
D.L. Underwood	1979	23	106	**14.85**

Roberts stunned the Indian batsmen on the tour that followed, taking thirty-two
wickets in the five Tests. Eight wickets came his way at Eden Gardens, before he
took 7-64 and 5-57 in the defeat at Chennai. Using his bouncer to great effect as
a wicket-taking delivery rather than just as a tool for intimidation, it was the most
productive series of his career.

He actually possessed two bouncers: a slower version, which encouraged batsmen
to hook; and the other, pitched in the same spot, was faster, often resulting in a
dismissal or – as Ian Botham found to his cost in a domestic game in 1974 – injury.

The summer of 1975 brought World Cup triumph for the West Indies, with Roberts playing his part, but it was with the bat that he made the headlines. Chasing 267 to win against Pakistan at Edgbaston, they still needed 64 when Roberts strode to the crease at number eleven to join Deryck Murray. They then proceeded to tick off the runs with minimum fuss to bring a one-wicket victory, with Roberts unbeaten on 24. It remains the highest tenth wicket partnership to win any ODI.

Runs	Partners	Match	Venue	Year
64*	**D.L. Murray & A.M.E. Roberts**	**West Indies v Pakistan**	**Birmingham**	**1975**
57*	J.P. Faulkner & C.J. McKay	Australia v England	Brisbane	2014
55*	T.M. Odoyo & H.A. Varaiya	Kenya v Ireland	Nairobi – R	2007
35*	Naeem Islam & Nazmul Hossain	Bangladesh v Zimbabwe	Chittagong – D	2009
32*	Abdul Razzaq & Shoaib Akhtar	Pakistan v South Africa	Abu Dhabi	2010

The West Indies were humiliated 5-1 in Australia the following season, but Roberts enabled the solitary victory in the series by taking 7-54 at Perth. That series defeat led Clive Lloyd to turn his attention to finding a battery of fast bowlers, and in Roberts he found his spearhead.

He took ten wickets at Lord's on the 1976 'grovel' tour and bowled a furious spell to David Steele, Frank Hayes and Chris Balderstone at Headingley. However, at the peak of his powers he signed for Kerry Packer's World Series Cricket and didn't play any more Test cricket until 1979, by which time he had signed for Leicestershire and injuries had started to catch up with him.

He was no longer as fast as he had been in his pomp, but in its place was intelligence. He took eight wickets in the 1980 Trent Bridge Test and twenty-four wickets when India visited the Caribbean for a Test series in early 1983. His 3-32 in the World Cup final later that year looked as if it could bring a third trophy to the West Indies, but he couldn't produce another batting miracle as they lost to India by 43 runs at Lord's.

He only had one more season in him as his knee problems reared up again, and coupled with a back injury, his Test career ended with 202 wickets. That wasn't the end of his association with the game as he worked first as coach of the West Indies national team and then as groundsman at the Antigua Recreation Ground – ironically, one of the flattest batting pitches in the world.

Michael Holding   international career 1975–87

'There has never been a more elegant dealer of bowling death.' Piers Morgan

Possessing arguably the most fantastic nickname in cricket history – 'Whispering Death' – no one made bowling at the speed of light look as easy as Michael Holding. Even when caught on camera demolishing the stumps in Dunedin after a caught behind appeal had been turned down, the act was performed with such grace that it could almost be forgiven.

He played his first representative match at the age of 10 for his local Dunrobin Area team and started off as an off-spinner who could bat a bit! Once at Kingston College, he immediately shone in both cricket and athletics. His first school cricket captain was Sydney Headley – the youngest son of George Headley – and his Under-12 school high jump record of 1.50 metres still stands to this day.

His rise was meteoric, and he progressed into the Jamaica youth team and subsequently made his first-class debut for Jamaica while still just 18. In that first season he started to make a name for himself with some impressive performances against the touring Australians, but his lean physique made him injury-prone and it was nearly three years before he made his Test debut.

It was a baptism of fire down under in the 1975/76 season, as he took just ten wickets at 61.40 each in the 5-1 series defeat to Australia. However, perhaps it was apt that in the one Test the West Indies won – at Perth – Holding took four wickets in the first innings and was described by Rodney Marsh as the fastest bowler in the world. He continued to breathe fire against India, and his nineteen wickets cost just 19.89 each and precipitated early declarations in both innings by Bishan Bedi at Jamaica to save his lower order from potential injury.

In 1976, having taken 5-17 to help bowl England out for just 71 at Old Trafford in the Third Test, Holding saved his best for last as he performed one of the greatest fast-bowling feats of all time in the final Test at The Oval. On a pitch where the West Indies had piled up 687/8 declared, he tore through England's batting to take 8-92 and 6-57 bowling fast and straight, still the best match figures by a West Indian.

Bowling	Player	Against	Venue	Year
14-149	**M.A. Holding**	**England**	**The Oval**	**1976**
13-55	C.A. Walsh	New Zealand	Wellington	1995
13-121	S.T. Gabriel	Sri Lanka	St Lucia	2018
12-121	A.M.E. Roberts	India	Madras	1975
11-84	C.E.L. Ambrose	England	Port-of-Spain	1994

Together with teammates Roberts, Garner, Croft and Marshall, he formed the greatest pace attack the world had ever seen. He didn't have a bad series for the rest of his career, the one blot on his copybook being the ill-tempered tour of New Zealand in early 1980 when his high kick earned him headlines around the world.

The common misconception with the West Indian fast bowlers is that they dismissed you by bowling short. Of his 249 Test wickets, eighty-one — nearly a third — were dismissed bowled, and a further thirty-five were lbw. Together with his one hit-wicket dismissal, 47 per cent needed no help from any fielders, which showed his method worked irrespective of weather and pitch conditions.

An under-rated batsman who loved hitting the long ball, he struck six Test half-centuries and his thirty-six Test sixes comprised nearly a quarter of his Test runs. It remains the highest tally for any batsman who fell short of 1,000 Test runs. He also contributed 12 unbeaten runs as he and Viv Richards added an unbroken 106 for the final wicket in the Manchester ODI in 1984, which is still the record for that wicket.

Runs	Partners	Match	Venue	Year
106*	**I.V.A. Richards & M.A. Holding**	**West Indies v England**	**Manchester**	**1984**
103	Mohammad Amir & Saeed Ajmal	Pakistan v New Zealand	Abu Dhabi	2009
99*	R. Rampaul & K.A.J. Roach	West Indies v India	Visakhapatnam	2011
76	L. Ronchi & M.J. McClenaghan	New Zealand v South Africa	Mt Maunganui	2014
76	Yasir Shah & Mohammad Amir	Pakistan v England	Nottingham	2016

After his retirement, he ran a petrol station in his native Jamaica with some of his old Melbourne Cricket Club teammates before moving into commentary with the same grace that he ran to the wicket.

Curtly Ambrose   international career 1988–2000

'He didn't say much so you didn't know if he hated your guts.' Steve Waugh

Lurking under the headlines throughout his career with the catchphrase 'Curtly talk to no man', Ambrose has been making up for it since his retirement, and as bass player in first 'Dread and the Bald Head' and then 'Spirited', he entertains in a totally different way to his earlier career.

He grew up an avid basketball player – as befits someone standing more than 2 metres tall – the son of a carpenter in Antigua. He started playing cricket on the beach at the age of 17, but found the games too long compared to the time he could spend on a basketball court. However, he came across fellow Antiguan Andy Roberts, who was to play a key part in his development and acted as a mentor for the young Ambrose on his cricketing journey.

On the recommendation of Viv Richards, he spent a summer with Chester Boughton Hall in the Liverpool & District League in 1986, taking eighty-four wickets in twenty-two matches at less than ten apiece. The following year, he took 115 wickets for Heywood in the Central Lancashire League, before visiting England again in 1988, but this time as part of the West Indian touring party.

His first-class debut did not come until he was 22 years old, but after he broke Winston Benjamin's record of thirty-three wickets in a domestic season in 1987/88, he was thrown into a Test debut with Pakistan with just six matches behind him. Ironically, that match at Bourda would prove to be the only home Test defeat for the West Indies throughout the entire decade of the 1980s.

Joel Garner's retirement had left a giant-sized hole in the West Indian attack, and into that strode Ambrose. He took twenty-two cheap wickets on that 1988 tour and he was there to stay. Soon afterwards, he was ready to lead the line against England on their 1990 tour to the Caribbean.

At Bridgetown, England were chasing 356 to win but they were all out for 191, with Ambrose ending with his career-best figures of 8-45. He took the final five wickets in five overs without any assistance from the fielders. He was at it again on the same ground against South Africa two years later. The tourists needed 201 to win their first Test back from isolation and were sitting pretty at 122/2 at the end of the fourth day. It was not to be, as Ambrose ended with figures of 6-34 as South Africa were shot out for just 148.

Stunning though those efforts were, perhaps his most staggering spell of bowling came at the WACA in Perth in January 1993, when he took seven wickets for just one run in thirty-two deliveries. Six of the seven wickets were caught by the wicketkeeper or in the slips. A shell-shocked Australia fell to an innings defeat and Ambrose's thirty-three wickets equalled the record for any series between the two teams.

Player	Team	Season	Matches	Wickets	Avge
C.V. Grimmett	Australia	1930/31	5	33	17.96
A.K. Davidson	Australia	1960/61	4	33	18.54
C.E.L. Ambrose	**West Indies**	**1992/93**	**5**	**33**	**16.42**
J. Garner	West Indies	1983/84	5	31	16.87
G.D. McKenzie	Australia	1968/69	5	30	25.26
G.D. McGrath	Australia	1998/99	4	30	16.93

England felt the full force of another Ambrose magical spell on their next tour of the Caribbean at Port of Spain. They needed just 194 to win, but he took 6-22 in a 7.5 over spell on the fourth evening to reduce them to 40/8 at the close. The following morning, they were bowled out for just 46, the second-lowest total in their history.

Perhaps unfairly for him, his Test career concluded with a series defeat in England in 2000. He ended with 405 Test wickets at an average of just 20.99 runs apiece. An avid follower of stats, in that respect he was disappointed to finish just behind the averages of Malcolm Marshall (20.94) and Joel Garner (20.97), but his wicket tally outstripped them both and he finished as the leading wicket-taker for the West Indies against England.

Player	Matches	Wickets	Avge
C.E.L. Ambrose	**34**	**164**	**18.79**
C.A. Walsh	36	145	25.40
M.D. Marshall	26	127	19.18
G.S. Sobers	36	102	32.57
L.R. Gibbs	26	100	28.89

James Anderson   **international career 2003–**

'There have been some very good bowlers I have played with, but for pure out-and-out skill and ability, there is no doubt that Jimmy has been the best.' Alastair Cook

While James Anderson was a pupil at St Theodore High School, he was more interested in football, and his heroes were Ian Wright and Boris Becker. Indeed, before he had a growth spurt in his mid-teens, there was no inkling that the scorer for Burnley Second XI would end up as England's greatest international Test wicket-taker of all.

He broke into the Burnley First XI at the age of 15 and although he played a total of twelve matches, scored only 5 runs and took only nine wickets. His returns in the Lancashire League increased in 1999 and 2000, which pushed him into Lancashire's Second XI, for whom he took twenty-three cheap wickets in 2001. It all led to a first-team debut against Derbyshire towards the end of the season, when wicketkeeper Warren Hegg told him simply to 'bowl as fast as you can'.

He made eleven Championship appearances in 2002 before he was chosen for the England Academy trip to Australia, and before the winter was out, he found himself in the full England ODI team, bowling ten overs for just 12 runs against Australia at Adelaide. To this day, no England bowler has bowled more maidens in an ODI match.

Bowling	Player	Against	Venue	Year
12-6-11-4	J.A. Snow	East Africa	Birmingham	1975
10-6-12-1	**J.M. Anderson**	**Australia**	**Adelaide**	**2003**
12-6-15-4	M. Hendrick	Pakistan	Leeds	1979

A Test debut came in the summer of 2003, when he recovered from conceding 17 runs in his first over to take 5-73 against Zimbabwe at Lord's. However, England's fast-bowling coach Troy Cooley decided that his action put him at risk of injury, and suggested he changed. When he was laid low by a stress fracture to his back in 2006, he decided that he would revert to his original action and never looked back.

The 2008 tour of New Zealand was a watershed. After defeat in the First Test at Hamilton, Stephen Harmison and Matthew Hoggard, two heroes from the 2005 Ashes triumph, were dropped for the next Test at Wellington and replaced by Anderson and Stuart Broad. The remaining two Tests on the tour were won and over the next decade they became the most durable and productive seam bowling combination in Test history.

Bowlers	Team	Matches	Wickets
J.M. Anderson & S.C.J. Broad	**Eng**	120	**919**
C.E.L. Ambrose & C.A. Walsh	WI	95	**762**
Wasim Akram & Waqar Younis	Pak	61	**559**
J.H. Kallis & S.M. Pollock	SA	93	**547**

Anderson silenced his critics who claimed he couldn't perform as well away from home by taking twenty-four wickets in the victorious 2010/11 Ashes series, and bowled well in the UAE, Sri Lanka and India. As he grew older, he developed into the finest swing bowler in the world, opening the 2013 Ashes series with ten wickets at Trent Bridge, before taking thirty-seven against Sri Lanka and India the following summer.

His ODI career came to an end after England's early exit in the 2015 World Cup but he still ended as England's leading wicket-taker in that form of the game too. He was irresistible on the early summer pitches against Sri Lanka in 2016, especially at Headingley, where his ten wickets cost just 45 runs and he reached number one in the ICC Test bowling rankings for the first time. Even better was to come the following summer, when his thirty-nine wickets against South Africa and the West Indies came at just 14.10 apiece.

His batting had its moments too. He started his career with an England record fifty-four successive duck-less innings and he managed to save the opening Test in the 2009 Ashes with Monty Panesar at Cardiff. Most remarkable though was his innings of 81 against India at Trent Bridge in 2014, in which he shared a world-record tenth wicket partnership of 198 with Joe Root.

Having sailed past Ian Botham's previous England record of 383 Test wickets back in 2015, his next target was 500, which duly came at Lord's just two years later. Finally, with his last delivery of the 2018 summer against India, he clean bowled Mohammed Shami to go past Glenn McGrath's total of 563 and become the most prolific fast bowler of all.

Brian Statham   **international career 1951–65**

'It never mattered what you asked him to do, whether it was to come on for a few overs, to bowl until lunch, to bowl uphill or upwind. Whatever it was, he would take the ball and do it.' – Peter May

Known universally as 'George', Statham overcame a slow start to his career to end it with a stint as Test cricket's highest wicket-taker, and was one of the most beloved of all England Test cricketers.

Born in Gorton, near Manchester, his initial progress through the ranks was slow and gave no indication of the finished product he was to become. From Whitworth School First XI, he moved to Denton West Cricket Club in the North West League and then Stockport in the Central Lancashire League. At the time the leagues were the home of many overseas stars, and so he had the opportunity to test himself against the likes of Vijay Hazare and Vinoo Mankad.

While on National Service, he caught the eye of his sports NCO, Corporal Lazarus, who recommended him to the MCC, who in turn advised the youngster to approach Lancashire. They soon offered him a trial and within two weeks of reporting, he made his first-class debut on his eighteenth birthday. His open-chested action did not appeal to the purists, but they were soon won over after he took 5-18 against Somerset at Bath in just his fourth match.

Having impressed Yorkshire's Len Hutton in the 1950 Roses match, when injury struck the England side in New Zealand the following winter, it was Hutton who advised captain Freddie Brown to select the Lancashire quick, and he made his Test debut at Christchurch. His Test career was somewhat stop-start though, partly due to the presence of Alec Bedser, Fred Trueman and Trevor Bailey, but he continued to improve in county cricket, increasing his pace until he was a genuinely quick bowler.

It wasn't for another four years that he finally established himself in the Test team, and even then, he never played more than thirteen successive Tests due to a combination of injuries and selectorial indifference. He was frequently overshadowed by his fast-bowling colleagues, but he did have plenty of his own moments in the sun. He found the South Africans at Lord's particularly to his liking, taking 7-39 against them in 1955, and then eleven wickets in the match five years later.

For Lancashire he was supreme, ending with 1,816 first-class wickets for his home county at the extraordinary average of 15.12. But his crowning glory came at Adelaide on England's 1962/63 Ashes tour. When he had Barry Shepherd caught by Trueman in the gully, he went past tour Assistant Manager Alec Bedser's world record of 236 Test wickets.

Player	Team	Matches	Wickets	Avge
J.B. Statham	**Eng**	**66**	**241**	**24.02**
A.V. Bedser	Eng	51	**236**	24.89
F.S. Trueman	Eng	53	**234**	22.18
R. Benaud	Aus	58	**231**	26.46
R.R. Lindwall	Aus	61	**228**	23.03

He claimed he breakfasted on 'a fag, a cough and a cup of coffee', and throughout his career he suffered from toe problems, which meant that he frequently had a bloody sock sticking out from a hole cut in his left boot in an attempt to reduce the pressure when he landed. Nevertheless, no one took more first-class wickets at a better average. His overall average of 16.37 is the best of any of the top twenty wicket-takers in history, and among the top thirty, it is only bettered by Johnny Briggs, who bowled exclusively in the nineteenth century.

Player	Wickets	Avge
J. Briggs	2,221	**15.95**
J.B. Statham	**2,260**	**16.37**
W. Rhodes	4,204	**16.72**
C. Blythe	2,503	**16.81**
J.T. Hearne	3,061	**17.75**

Later in life he served as Lancashire's president, and one of the ends of the Old Trafford ground bears his name.

Alec Bedser   **international career 1946–55**

'He's the first bowler to be knighted since Sir Francis Drake.' – Eric Bedser

Inseparable from his twin brother Eric, the twins played their first cricket at the age of 7 before progressing to Monument Hill School and Woking Cricket Club. Leaving school at 14, they both joined a firm of solicitors in Lincoln's Inn Fields but continued to develop their skills at a cricket school in Woking. It was there they were spotted by former Surrey batsman Alan Peach, and in 1938 both joined the Surrey staff at The Oval.

It was then that their careers diverged – albeit slightly – as Eric decided to change from bowling seam to off breaks, reasoning that otherwise they might have competed for the same spot in the team. However, just a year later, and after Alec had played only two first-class games, war broke out and the twins were sent to France.

They were evacuated from Dunkirk in 1940, and went on to serve in North Africa, Italy and Austria. When not serving abroad, Alec played some cricket – impressing against the Australians, West Indies and the 'Dominions', against whom he played some one-day cricket in 1942 and 1943. The twins were demobilised in the spring of 1946, and so both were able to embark on their county careers.

Alec's Test career started in a blaze of glory at the age of nearly 28, with eleven wickets in each of his first two matches against India in 1946, setting a record for the best start by any England bowler in his first two matches.

Player	Wickets	Avge
A.V. Bedser	**22**	**10.81**
S.F. Barnes	**19**	15.89
A.E. Trott	**17**	11.64
N.G.B. Cook	**17**	16.17
J.D.F. Larter	**16**	13.87
T. Richardson	**16**	22.75

In his early days he frequently ploughed a lone furrow for England in terms of seam bowling, with eleven bowlers sharing the new ball with him, including a pair of 38-year-olds in Bill Bowes and Bill Voce at the start of his career. As England struggled for Test victories in the 1940s, Bedser was the shining light with the ball and gave a hint of better times ahead.

He did not possess great pace, but he could surprise the batsman and was a master of late inswing. Wicketkeepers often stood up to him, and he was helped by having Godfrey Evans keep to him for the majority of his England career. When Lindwall and Miller ruined England batting on the 1946/47 Ashes tour, Bedser needed something to try to counteract the Don Bradman-inspired Australian run-scoring. He developed a leg cutter that he used to great effect, most notably at Adelaide when he bowled Bradman for a duck with what the batsman considered the best ball he ever received.

He took thirty wickets in each of the 1950/51 Ashes and 1951 home series against South Africa, and when Trueman, Bailey and Statham came on the scene to take some pressure from his shoulders, he helped England to their memorable 1953 Ashes victory with thirty-nine wickets, setting an England Ashes record at the time, which only one bowler has bettered since then.

Player	Season	Matches	Wickets	Avge
J.C. Laker	1956	5	46	9.60
A.V. Bedser	**1953**	**5**	**39**	**17.48**
M.W. Tate	1924/25	5	38	23.18
S.F. Barnes	1911/12	5	34	22.88
I.T. Botham	1981	6	34	20.58

He started with fourteen wickets at Nottingham and eight more at Lord's. Seven followed in each of the Manchester and Leeds matches, in the latter of which he went past the world record of 216 wickets held by Clarrie Grimmett. His dominance over Arthur Morris became a huge talking point as he dismissed the Australian opener eighteen times in twenty-one Tests.

Later in life he was an England selector for twenty-four years – as chairman for thirteen of those years – and was knighted for services to cricket. And throughout his life he stayed together with his twin brother Eric. Neither married and they often dressed alike, adding to the confusion.

Tom Richardson   **international career 1893–98**

'In his prime he presented as handsome a sight as ever seen on a cricket field. Dark black haired, black moustached and twinkling gipsy eyes.' Neville Cardus

Tom Richardson was born in Byfleet, in Surrey, in 1870, but by the time he was 11 his family had moved to Mitcham and the young Tom was playing cricket on the green. Even at that tender age it was apparent that he had a gift for the game, and he took 102 wickets for Mitcham in 1891 at an average of just 7 runs apiece. Therefore, it was no surprise when he joined Surrey the following year.

He was a workhorse, with a willingness to pound away all day, not merely for a few overs with the new ball, and took over as Surrey's spearhead when George Lohmann's health started to decline. He didn't just put in a supreme effort on the pitch, but he would walk the 7 miles from his home to The Oval every day and back again at the close of play – a total of 14 miles – all while carrying his kit bag.

His Test career started with a bang as he took ten Australian wickets at Old Trafford in 1893, and his bowling average of 10.32 for his 196 wickets in the 1894 season remains the best for anyone taking at least 100 first-class wickets in an English season since the County Championship was first held as an official competition in 1890.

Player	Season	Matches	Wickets	Avge
T. Richardson	**1894**	**23**	**196**	**10.32**
H.L. Jackson	1958	26	143	**10.99**
H.J. Rhodes	1965	24	119	**11.04**
J.T. Hearne	1891	18	129	**11.23**
W. Rhodes	1923	37	134	**11.54**

His excellent physique enabled him to maintain his long run-up through the longest of spells and his high arm enabled him to deliver his key weapon, which was a fast off break. He was able to translate his success to Australia, taking thirty-two wickets in the 1894/95 series and a further twenty-two when he returned three years later.

At his peak he was one of the greatest of all fast bowlers and he took a staggering 809 first-class wickets in the three seasons of 1895, 1896 and 1897, with his tally of 290 in the first of those years remaining a record for thirty-three years and is still the highest by any pace bowler.

His performances in the 1896 Ashes series became the stuff of legend. Having won the Lord's Test with eleven wickets, he then took 7-168 and 6-76 in the next Test at Old Trafford in one of the greatest of all fast-bowling efforts. On a featherbed of a wicket, he bowled sixty-eight overs in the first innings and then bowled unchanged for three hours, delivering 42.3 overs in the second innings as Australia sneaked home by three wickets.

Years of over-bowling started to take their toll and he was never quite the same from 1899 onwards as heavy drinking and injuries also affected his body. However, in 1903 he reached 2,000 first-class wickets in the fewest number of matches of any bowler, to go with his 1,000 wicket speed record – both marks that still stand to this day.

Player	Matches to 1,000	Player	Matches to 2,000
T. Richardson	133	T. Richardson	326
F.W. Lillywhite	143	J.T. Hearne	347
E.G. Dennett	147	E.G. Dennett	348
A.W. Mold	149	A.P. Freeman	350
W.R. Hillyer	149	C. Blythe	350

Alas, his congenital heart abnormality – which had resulted in his rejection from both the police and the army earlier in his life – culminated in a fatal heart attack when walking in France at the age of just 41.

Allan Donald   international career 1992–2003

'He was a fearsome sight for opposition batsmen – the long, loping run, the athletic follow-through and always a touch of war-paint thrown into the mix.' Michael Atherton

Born in Bloemfontein in Free State, Allan Donald first made his name as a fast but wild bowler while attending Hoër Tegniese Skool Louis Botha. Despite the school concentrating more on rugby, he was picked to represent South African Schools in 1985, speaking hardly a word of English.

A first-class debut for Free State followed in November that year against the mighty Transvaal side; it was a difficult experience, which ended in an innings defeat thanks to the efforts of Clive Rice, Graeme Pollock, Neal Radford and Hugh Page. Donald did pick up a first wicket though, and it wasn't a bad one – Jimmy Cook.

He fared somewhat better against the same Transvaal team when they met at the Wanderers in January 1987, taking 8-37 in the first innings, which propelled him at the age of just 20 into the South African side to face Kim Hughes' Australian 'rebel' side the following week. And that summer he became the beneficiary of a friendship made some twenty years earlier.

When South Africa had toured England in 1965, Ali Bacher became friendly with Warwickshire's David Brown. Fast forward to 1987, and Brown was the manager at Warwickshire and Donald was given a year's trial at the county – for a salary of £6,000. It was the start of a relationship with the club that went far beyond the eleven years he spent playing for them, in the early years of which there was some talk of him qualifying for England.

His first few years at Warwickshire helped him reach his peak at the right time. However, his Test debut – when it finally came – proved a chastening one. In South Africa's first Test back at Bridgetown in April 1992, he took 4-77 in the West Indies second innings to ensure South Africa's target was an achievable 201. At 122-2 at the end of day four they were cruising, but Curtly Ambrose and Courtney Walsh had other ideas. The final eight wickets clattered for just 25 runs the following morning, with Donald the last man out – bowled first ball by Ambrose.

However, after that start his career went from strength to strength as he became the first South African to take 300 Test wickets. Of all his countrymen with at least 150 wickets in the longest form of the game, he has the best average – although it is tight at the top.

Player	Matches	Wickets	Avge
A.A. Donald	72	330	**22.25**
V.D. Philander	64	224	**22.32**
D.W. Steyn	93	439	**22.95**
K. Rabada	43	197	**22.95**
S.M. Pollock	108	421	**23.11**

His ferocious battle with England's Michael Atherton at Trent Bridge in 1998 has lived long in the memory, and he took a total of eighty wickets in his fourteen Tests that year to set a national record.

Player	Year	Matches	Wickets
A.A. Donald	**1998**	**14**	**80**
D.W. Steyn	2008	13	**74**
S.M. Pollock	1998	14	**69**
D.W. Steyn	2010	11	**60**
M. Ntini	2003	12	**59**

In their early years after readmission, South Africa's victories came primarily from their bowling rather than their batting, and Donald was responsible as much as anyone. He was able to successfully bridge the gap between the wilderness years and the modern succession of pace bowlers produced by the South Africans.

Despite taking more than 600 wickets in international cricket, it is possibly as a batsman that he made one of his lasting impressions. It was he who was run out at the non-striker's end in the famous 1999 World Cup semi-final tied match, which saw Australia progress to the final and leave South Africa still waiting for their first appearance in the title match.

Ray Lindwall   **international career 1946–60**

'Poetry.' Pelham Warner

Before Michael Holding came along in the 1970s, there was Ray Lindwall. His run-up was poetry in motion, and he was one of the fastest bowlers in the world at his peak, delivering the ball at the end of a long final stride at a low-slung 45 degrees. His stock ball was the late outswinger, but his action made bouncers even more challenging.

Growing up, he and his friends would bowl at paraffin tins in the very street in Hurstville that Bill O'Reilly used to walk along to try to catch his eye. At the age of 11 he was inspired by watching Harold Larwood on the 'Bodyline' tour, and at the age of 15, he scored a double-century and a century on the same day in club matches. The following year, he joined O'Reilly's club, St George's, and the Australian spinner played a key role in the young Lindwall's development.

A natural athlete, Lindwall could have turned his hand to any number of sports. He could run a hundred yards in less than eleven seconds, he was a fine swimmer and an excellent rugby league full back. But to the delight of cricket fans and the eventual dismay of opposing batsmen the world over, he chose cricket.

He earned a debut for New South Wales against Queensland in November 1941, but that would be his last action on a first-class cricket field for four long years. He found a worthwhile use of his wartime service in New Guinea and the Solomon Islands by marking up his run-up between two palm trees and repeatedly rehearsing his action for when peace would come.

On his return, an innings of 134 at number nine against Queensland proved his batting prowess and he was given a Test debut alongside his mentor O'Reilly against New Zealand. However, it was during the 1946/47 series against England that he established himself as a star. He took 7-63 in England's first innings at Sydney, and his century in the New Year's Test at Melbourne remained the fastest Australian Ashes hundred for nearly sixty years.

Player	Venue	Year	Balls
A.C. Gilchrist	Perth	2006	57
R.R. Lindwall	**Melbourne**	**1947**	**88**
A.C. Gilchrist	Sydney	2003	94
S.R. Watson	Perth	2013	106
J.M. Gregory	Melbourne	1921	109

He led the attack on the all-conquering 1948 tour of England, taking twenty-seven wickets in the Test series at an average of just 19.62 apiece. The final Test at The Oval is forever remembered as Bradman's farewell, but Lindwall's domination of the opposition batsmen culminated in him taking 6-20 as England were dismissed for just 52. He was still at the top of his game when he returned in 1953, taking twenty-six wickets in the series, even though it ended in defeat.

For a man whose bouncers – such as the one that felled Denis Compton at Old Trafford in 1948 – often made the headlines, a glance at his statistics reveals that more than 42 per cent of all his Test wickets were dismissed bowled, with a further 14 per cent leg-before.

He was still opening the bowling at the age of 38 and became the first Australian pace bowler to capture more than 200 Test wickets.

Player	Against	Venue	Year
R.R. Lindwall	**Pakistan**	**Karachi**	**1956**
G.D. McKenzie	West Indies	Melbourne	1968
D.K. Lillee	England	Melbourne	1980
J.R. Thomson	England	Edgbaston	1985
M.G. Hughes	England	Headingley	1993

Like his successor Dennis Lillee, once his electrifying pace had dwindled, he more than made up for it with intelligence and expertise in technique. He once saw the young Alan Davidson bowl a bouncer at an opposing number eight. 'You've admitted a number eight can bat better than you can bowl,' Lindwall said. 'Get into the nets and learn how to bowl.' And so he took him there, and taught him, and he ended up doing all right too!

Fred Spofforth   international career 1877–87

'His delivery was terrifying, for he came to the wicket, a long lean man, all arms and legs, and all apparently making amazing evolutions.' Lord Hawke

Fred Spofforth achieved his legendary status by being perhaps the first aggressive fast bowler in Test history, culminating in his great feats of 1882, when he bowled Australia to victory in the Oval Test that caused the Ashes to be born. It could have been the other way around as his father Edward left Yorkshire for Australia in 1836.

After spending some of his childhood in New Zealand, he returned to Sydney and attended Eglinton College before starting work as a clerk in the Bank of New South Wales. However, cricket played a major part in his life and having changed from fast underarm to fast overarm at the age of 11, he started playing for Toxteth Cricket Club.

His first successes came for the Albert Club in Sydney and he took nine wickets for just 10 runs against Sydney University, which helped gain selection for the New South Wales XVIII against W.G. Grace's touring England team in January 1874. When England returned three years later for the first Test match, he had made his name as a bowler, but he didn't play: rumour had it that he refused since his great friend Billy Murdoch had not been selected to keep wicket.

However fast he may have been, his first Test wicket came by way of a stumping, pouring scorn on Spofforth's claims that he was the fastest bowler who ever lived! However, he was a master of variation in terms of swing, spin and position on the crease. Without any change in his action he could deliver the ball faster or slower, and his glare was quite possibly the first example of intimidation from bowler to batsman.

It was on the 1878 tour of England that his reputation was made. Australia won eight matches on that tour, and he played a major part in most. He took twelve wickets against the Players and against Gloucestershire, eleven against Surrey and – most impressively – ten against the MCC, who were pretty much a full England side. His figures of 6-4 and 4-16 helped the tourists rout their hosts in just a single day in which 105 runs were scored for the loss of thirty-one wickets, still the lowest aggregate in a completed first-class match in history.

Aggregate	Match	Venue	Year
105	**MCC v Australians**	**Lord's**	**1878**
134	Kent v Sussex	Hawkhurst	1826
134	England v The Bs	Lord's	1831
147	Kent v Sussex	Sevenoaks	1828
149	England v Kent	Lord's	1858

On 2 January 1879, Spofforth took the first hat-trick in Test cricket and ended with thirteen wickets in the match at Melbourne. He toured England again in 1880, by which time he acquired the nickname 'the Demon', but a broken finger kept him out of the Test match. He made up for it in 1882, when his fourteen wickets at The Oval rescued Australia when England needed only 85 to win.

He took 207 wickets on the 1884 tour before marrying and settling in Derbyshire as well as playing for Hampstead Cricket Club. He wrote for magazines and had a reputation as a great raconteur – even if some of his stories were a little 'tall'. Emphasising how great he was, more than a hundred years after his last match, he still has two of the best five match bowling analyses in Test matches for Australia.

Bowling	Player	Against	Venue	Year
16-137	R.A.L. Massie	England	Lord's	1972
14-90	**F.R. Spofforth**	**England**	**The Oval**	**1882**
14-199	C.V. Grimmett	South Africa	Adelaide	1932
13-77	M.A. Noble	England	Melbourne	1902
13-110	**F.E. Spofforth**	**England**	**Melbourne**	**1879**

Shaun Pollock   international career 1995–2008

'He's an icon, he's up there with South Africa's greatest cricketers.' Graeme Smith

Few players have been lucky enough to have been born into such a rich gene pool as Shaun Pollock. His father was Peter, who was one of South Africa's finest fast bowlers, and uncle Graeme ended his short Test career with a batting average of more than 60. Young Shaun was born three years too late to see his father and uncle help the all-conquering 1970 South African side lay waste to Bill Lawry's tourists to the tune of a 4-0 series whitewash. A name that could have been a millstone around his neck proved nothing of the sort as he graduated into one of the game's greatest bowlers.

He represented every age group growing up, from junior school to high school to university, and was picked for the South Africa Schools Week at the age of 18. The following year came a first-class debut for Natal, and he first crossed paths with the man who was to become his inspiration.

Malcolm Marshall signed to play for Natal in the 1992/93 season and his methodical attitude and ability to think a batsman out rubbed off on his teammates, who included Pollock, Jonty Rhodes and Lance Klusener.

Pollock delivered the ball from as high as he could, with an upright action, and bowled incredibly wicket to wicket – occasionally dislodging a stump at the bowler's end as he bowled. With the bat he was correct, occasionally capable of playing an explosive innings, and he ended his career with a Test batting average of 32 to accompany his bowling average of twenty-three.

When he was young, the only international visitors to his shores were rebel sides, but the return to the sporting fold was perfect timing for the younger Pollock, and he debuted in the 1995/96 Test series with England, in which he took sixteen wickets and averaged 26.60 with the bat. At least he was able to justify his position given that his father was the convenor of selectors at the time! On his ODI debut in the same series, he scored 66 not out and took 4-34 – just the third player to score a half-century and take four wickets on his ODI debut.

Player	Batting	Bowling	Match	Venue	Year
D.A.G. Fletcher	69*	4-42	Zimbabwe v Australia	Nottingham	1983
G.J. Crocker	50	4-26	Zimbabwe v India	Harare	1992
S.M. Pollock	**66***	**4-34**	**South Africa v England**	**Cape Town**	**1996**

Pollock and Allan Donald played forty-seven Tests together and South Africa only lost nine of them. Never one to resort to sledging, he remains to this day the nicest man you could ever hope to meet. He took over the captaincy at one of its darkest hours – in the shadow of Hansie Cronje – and led South Africa to victory in the Caribbean, but it was the 2003 World Cup disappointment on home soil that led to his eventual replacement by Graeme Smith.

He was made one of the scapegoats for the performance, especially the tied match against Sri Lanka that sealed their elimination, and he was asked to resign. He refused, so he was fired instead. However, he played another forty Tests and 117 ODIs after his removal from the captaincy until his retirement after a Test against the West Indies on his home ground of Durban.

He enjoyed successful county spells in England, marking his Warwickshire debut in 1996 by taking four wickets in four balls. He was also the first South African to take 400 Test wickets and became the first player to achieve the 3,000 run/300 wicket double in both Test and ODI cricket. When he finally called it a day, he was – and remains – the leading wicket-taker for South Africa in all international cricket. The pressure of the name clearly encouraged rather than overawed him.

Player	Matches	Wickets
S.M. Pollock	414	823
D.W. Steyn	262	695
M. Ntini	283	661
A.A. Donald	236	602
J.H. Kallis	513	572

Courtney Walsh   international career 1984–2001

'There has never been a more durable pace man, or a more wholehearted one.'
Vic Marks

In the 1927 musical *Show Boat* you can hear the song *Ol' Man River*, written by Jerome Kern and Oscar Hammerstein, which contrasts the hardships of the slaves with the flow of the Mississippi River through their homeland. It could have been written about Courtney Walsh, as he just kept rolling along.

Perhaps the last of the great breed of West Indian fast bowlers stretching pretty much back to their first Test match in 1928, he debuted as the fourth seamer alongside Marshall, Garner and Holding, and was still bowling quickly seventeen years later when he took his Test bow with 519 wickets, more wickets than any of his countrymen.

Player	Matches	Wickets	Avge
C.A. Walsh	**132**	**519**	**24.44**
C.E.L. Ambrose	98	**405**	20.99
M.D. Marshall	81	**376**	20.94
L.R. Gibbs	79	**309**	29.09
J. Garner	58	**259**	20.97

He played his early cricket for Melbourne Cricket Club in Jamaica – the club also represented by Michael Holding – and started life as a leg-spinner. It was only on the suggestion of the captain, Carlton Carter Jr, that he gave up spin bowling and concentrated on bowling quickly. His strong showing in the 1983/84 domestic season earned him not only a call-up for the 1984 tour of England, but a deal with Gloucestershire, as he had been spotted by Tom Graveney, who liked what he saw.

He was unable to break into the West Indies first team on that tour of England, but he played all five Tests against Australia that winter, taking thirteen wickets. Once in England for Gloucestershire, he was a revelation, taking eighty-five wickets for the county in 1985, and the following year he was the leading wicket-taker in the country with 118 as the county narrowly failed to win the County Championship for the first time. On four other occasions he topped the season wicket-takers' list.

Come the retirements of the elder statesmen of the West Indian team, Walsh started to move up through the ranks. His open-chested action helped him to stay relatively injury-free for the duration of his career and he developed a mystifying slower ball.

As the rest of the supporting cast fell by the wayside, he formed a superb partnership with Curtly Ambrose towards the end of his career, which brought many a nightmare for opposing batsmen even as the team descended from the incredible heights of the mid-1990s to the startling lows of the early 2000s.

He wasn't as fast as some of his contemporaries and he wasn't as menacing as others, and it took him twelve Tests before he picked up his first five-wicket haul. However, he kept going longer and bowled more deliveries than any pace bowler before him. When his age started to creep up, he concentrated on unerring accuracy and length, with substantial sideways movement off the seam.

His batting was comical at best and his forty-three ducks remain a Test record. However, among the slogs he memorably survived five deliveries as Brian Lara scripted a famous one-wicket win against Australia at Bridgetown in 1999.

Player	Team	Ducks	Innings
C.A. Walsh	**WI**	**43**	**185**
C.S. Martin	NZ	**36**	104
G.D. McGrath	Aus	**35**	138
S.C.J. Broad	Eng	**35**	208
S.K. Warne	Aus	**34**	199

The Test bowling record has been pushed upwards past 600, 700 and, finally, to 800 wickets. However, Courtney Walsh will always be remembered for being the first to 500.

Maurice Tate   international career 1924–35

'Maurice was one of the greatest bowlers of all time. It is difficult to find words to praise him sufficiently. I know from experience how difficult it was to play against him.' Jack Hobbs

Twenty bowlers have taken a wicket with their first ball in Test cricket and a very mixed bunch they are too. South Africa's Hardus Viljoen is still waiting for his second, and New Zealand's Dennis Smith's dismissal of Eddie Paynter also proved to be his only wicket in the only Test he played. At the other end of the scale come Nathan Lyon, who is Australia's third-most successful bowler, and England's Maurice Tate, with 155. But that only tells part of the story.

Tate's father Fred dropped a crucial catch and had been the last man out as England lost the 1902 Old Trafford Test by just 3 runs. However, legend has it that he claimed that he had a son who would put things right, and how right he was.

Maurice joined Sussex as a 15-year-old, primarily as a net bowler but impressed enough to be given a first-class debut just two years later. He played eight matches in the 1914 season but averaged just 15.12 with the bat and took only ten wickets, and it was only when Surrey suggested that he might join them once the war had ended that Sussex decided to retain his services.

He started as a slow bowler like his father, but in 1922 changed to seam bowling completely by chance after sending down a quicker delivery in the nets on an off day and demolishing the batsman's stumps. He stuck with the new style and took eight wickets against Kent in his first match. He never looked back and after taking five wickets without conceding a run in the 1923 Test Trial, he started his Test career with a bang the following summer as he and captain Arthur Gilligan routed South Africa for just 30 at Edgbaston.

He was a revelation on the subsequent Ashes Tour of Australia, bowling as many overs as any two of his other teammates combined. His thirty-eight wickets set a record for any Ashes series and remain a record for England in Australia.

Player	Season	Matches	Wickets	Avge
M.W. Tate	**1924/25**	**5**	**38**	**23.18**
S.F. Barnes	1911/12	5	**34**	22.88
H. Larwood	1932/33	5	**33**	19.51
F.R. Foster	1911/12	5	**32**	21.62
T. Richardson	1894/95	5	**32**	26.53

He possessed a superb command of length and is credited with having been the first bowler to take advantage of the seam, making the ball either break back or go away. He helped England retain the Ashes in the summer of 1926, but found things more difficult to take on his next tour of Australia in 1928/29, at one stage going 952 deliveries between wickets. He did continue to bowl economically, and to this day, no one has taken more Test wickets and conceded fewer runs per over.

With a total of 2,784 first-class wickets to his name, his batting feats are often overlooked, and on three occasions he performed the 'double' of 1,000 first-class runs and 200 first-class wickets in the same season, more times than anyone else.

Player	Team	Seasons
M.W. Tate	**Sussex**	3
A.E. Trott	Middlesex	2
G.H. Hirst	Yorkshire	1
A.S. Kennedy	Lancashire	1

Kapil Dev   international career 1978–94

'There is something reminiscent of a wild animal in the sight of Kapil Dev on the cricket field. He is a restless figure, erect and alert, saucer eyes darting hither and thither, muscles, it seems, twitching like a deer on the lookout for danger.'
Christopher Martin-Jenkins

Above all else, Kapil Dev was the man who made India really believe they could compete – and achieve – at the very highest level. Their triumph in the World Cup final in 1983 against the twice defending champions West Indies created a seismic shift in cricket still felt to this day. Kapil's catch from a Viv Richards top edge was instrumental in that 1983 victory and is still talked about today as one of the great catches in cricket history. Earlier in that competition, his astonishing unbeaten 175 against Zimbabwe at Tunbridge Wells rescued his side from 17 for five and enabled them to win the match by 31 runs.

He was born in Chandigarh and at the age of 12 was taken under the wing of Desh Azad, a former first-class cricketer-turned coach. It was to prove a lifelong association, and Kapil credited his coach for teaching him discipline and honesty on the field, as well as helping him to perfect his all-round skills.

He made his first-class debut for Haryana in November 1975 at the age of just 16 and struck an unbeaten 26, batting at number eleven, before taking 6-39 to bowl Punjab out for just 63. That proved to be a taste of things to come as three years later, he took the field for India in a Test for the first time.

He came on the scene when the Indian new ball was shared by Solkar, Amarnath and Gavaskar before being handed to any of the famous quartet of spinners to do their thing. Fast bowlers were not traditionally produced by India, but Kapil bucked that trend. In just over a year, at the age of 21, he had completed the 1,000 run/100 wicket double, the shortest time achieved by anyone, and a record that still stands.

Time	Player	Team	Matches
1y 105d	**Kapil Dev**	**Ind**	**25**
2y 33d	I.T. Botham	Eng	21
2y 257d	A.W. Greig	Eng	37
2y 327d	M.G. Johnson	Aus	37
3y 10d	S.M. Pollock	SA	26

He was a raw talent at the start, when he often tried to bowl as quickly as he could and hit the ball as far as possible, but with time he refined his skills. Suddenly, India had a fast bowler who could dismiss the opposition with pace and swing. Never was this better demonstrated than at the MCG in 1981, when he took 5-28 to bowl Australia out for just 83 and bring a miraculous Indian victory by 59 runs.

His batting was full of natural flair. No one will forget his four successive sixes off Eddie Hemmings in 1990, which landed in the building site from which would rise the Compton and Edrich stands at Lord's. The fact that they occurred when his side needed exactly 24 runs to avoid the follow-on added to the magic. That record has been equalled since then, but not surpassed.

Sixes	Batsman	Bowler	Match	Venue	Year
4	**Kapil Dev**	**E.E. Hemmings**	**India v England**	**Lord's**	**1990**
4	Shahid Afridi	Harbhajan Singh	Pakistan v India	Lahore	2006
4	AB de Villiers	A.B. McDonald	South Africa v Australia	Cape Town	2009

He could hold his own with the other three leading all-rounders who made the 1980s such a memorable decade, but his longevity meant that he ended up with more runs and wickets than all his famous all-round competitors. His whole country rejoiced when he took his 432nd Test wicket to take him past Richard Hadlee's world record, and he retired soon afterwards having taken 219 of his wickets on unforgiving Indian pitches. He gave hope to a new generation of seamers that wickets could be taken in those conditions, and the current crop of Indian pace bowlers can all count Kapil Dev as their main inspiration.

Wes Hall   international career 1958–69

'Hall had a magnificent, bounding approach, eyes bulging, teeth glinting, crucifix flying, climaxing in a classical cartwheel action and intimidating follow-through.'
David Frith

Astonishing to relate, the man who bowled arguably the most famous two overs in Test history started out as a wicketkeeper at Combermere School. After leaving school, he started work at Cable & Wireless, and represented their cricket club. One day, their regular opening bowler couldn't make the game against Wanderers and so Hall was given the new ball. He took six wickets and that was the end of his wicketkeeping career.

The West Indies selectors clearly saw something they liked because after just one wicket-less first-class match, he was fast-tracked into the national squad to tour England in 1957 at the age of just 19. His fifteen matches on that tour saw him take only twenty-seven wickets and not only didn't he feature in any of the Tests, but he was dropped for the subsequent series against Pakistan.

Luck came his way the following year when Frank Worrell had to withdraw from the 1958/59 tour of India and Pakistan and Hall replaced him, which proved a revelation. He took seven wickets in the opening tour match against Baroda and was promoted to take the new ball in the Test series with Roy Gilchrist. In the Second Test at Kanpur he took 6-50 and 5-76, which secured his place as the leader of the West Indies attack for the next decade.

He finished the tour with forty-six wickets in eight Tests and at Lahore he became the first of only four West Indian bowlers to take a hat-trick in a Test.

Player	Against	Venue	Year
W.W. Hall	**Pakistan**	**Lahore**	**1959**
L.R. Gibbs	Australia	Adelaide	1961
C.A. Walsh	Australia	Brisbane	1988
J.J.C. Lawson	Australia	Bridgetown	2003

He added a further twenty-two wickets in five Tests against England at the start of 1960, which included figures of 7-69 at Kingston and 6-90 at Georgetown. That performance earned him a three-year stint with Accrington in the Lancashire League, in which he took more than a hundred wickets each season and twice took all ten wickets in an innings.

At the end of his first season at Accrington, the West Indies headed for Australia for what became arguably the greatest Test series ever. Having already bowled seventeen eight-ball overs on the final day of the opening Test at Brisbane, he prepared to bowl the last over of the match, with Australia needing 6 to win with three wickets in hand. Seven deliveries, 5 runs, a wicket and two run-outs later, Test cricket had its first tie, and Hall earned himself an invitation to play a couple of seasons for Queensland.

He took twenty-seven wickets at just 15.74 each as India were crushed 5-0 in early 1962, and later that year, he became the first of seven West Indian bowlers to reach the number one spot in the ICC Test bowling rankings.

Player	Date
W.W. Hall	**Dec 1962**
A.M.E. Roberts	**Jul 1976**
J. Garner	**Jan 1981**
L.R. Gibbs	**Mar 1981**
M.A. Holding	**Feb 1982**
M.D. Marshall	**Dec 1984**
C.E.L. Ambrose	**Jul 1991**

His stamina was also evident at the end of the 1963 Lord's Test. Hall had broken Colin Cowdrey's arm the previous day but with England nine wickets down, Cowdrey strolled to the non-striker's end with two balls left and England needing 6 to win. Into the final over of a marathon 200-minute spell either side of tea, Hall's last two deliveries were dealt with by David Allen and the match ended in a draw.

He was instrumental in the first series victory for the West Indies over Australia, taking nine wickets at Port of Spain in the 2-1 triumph in the 1964/65 season and chipped in with eighteen wickets as the West Indies won a 3-1 series victory in England in 1966.

His years of hostile bowling combined with a long run-up finally caught up with him before the following tour of India, when he suffered a knee injury, and his international performances tailed off from then on. Alas, he limped from the field against New Zealand in Auckland in 1969 in what was to be his final Test appearance.

Not one to enjoy a quiet retirement, he threw himself into politics, serving in Barbados's cabinet for a decade, and was ordained by the church. In 2012, he was knighted for services to sport and the community, and remained one of the most loved players ever produced by the West Indies.

Chapter 6
Slow Bowlers

Shane Warne   international career 1992–2007

'Warne swaggered down the middle of the road, living large but always bowling big, revelling in the attention while never losing the love of his craft, seeming to treat the tabloid exposés as sixes hit off his bowling. Just an occupational hazard.'
Gideon Haigh

Possibly the most charismatic cricketer of modern times, Shane Warne made bowling leg spin cool again. Australia had a proud history of leg-spinners, most notably Bill O'Reilly, Clarrie Grimmett and Richie Benaud. But there had been a lull before he exploded on the scene in the early 1990s to cast a spell on batsmen worldwide.

Prior to making his Test debut, Warne had taken only twenty-six first-class wickets, of which only fifteen had been in Australia. He struggled early, with his bowling average peaking at 346 before his three quick wickets hastened Sri Lanka to defeat in Colombo in late 1992.

That average was still in three figures before he took 7-52 against the West Indies in the 1992 Boxing Day Test. Then came the 'Ball of the Century' at Manchester, and by the time he had finished, he had taken more wickets against England than any other bowler.

Player	Team	Matches	Wickets
S.K. Warne	**Aus**	**36**	**195**
D.K. Lillee	Aus	29	**167**
C.E.L. Ambrose	WI	34	**164**
G.D. McGrath	Aus	30	**157**
C.A. Walsh	WI	36	**145**

He took more than 200 wickets in his next forty Tests, and that was when he was at the peak of his powers. A finger operation in 1996 and a shoulder operation two years later meant that his flipper was not as lethal as it had been earlier in his career. However, he more than made up for it through intelligence, the finer arts of gamesmanship and psychological warfare. He didn't go wicket-less in any of his last sixty-three Tests from 2000, in which time he made some of the greatest names in the game look like amateurs.

Alec Stewart was famously bamboozled by his flipper, Andrew Strauss padded up outside his off stump and the ball cannoned into his leg stump, Graham Gooch was bowled around his legs and Basit Ali was bowled between his legs. Warne's continued mastery over Darryl Cullinan sent the South African batsman to a psychologist to try to unravel his mysteries.

A key part of the Australian side that won the 1999 World Cup, Warne took twenty wickets in the competition and was named 'Player of the Match' in both the semi-final and the final. It was a different story four years later as he was sent home from the 2003 tournament in South Africa in disgrace, having tested positive for a banned substance.

No mean batsman, he is the holder of the record for the most Test runs without ever scoring a century, with a highest score of 99 against New Zealand at Perth in 2001, which ended with his dismissal to a 'non-called' Daniel Vettori no-ball.

Player	Team	Matches	Runs	HS
S.K. Warne	**Aus**	**145**	**3,154**	**99**
C.P.S. Chauhan	Ind	40	**2,084**	97
D.L. Murray	WI	62	**1,993**	91
D.P.D.N. Dickwella	SL	37	**1,921**	83
M.D. Marshall	WI	81	**1,810**	92

He was also a fine slip fielder, perhaps unluckily remembered more for his dropping of Kevin Pietersen at The Oval in 2005 than for any blinders he may have caught. However, without his forty wickets and 249 runs in the series, it wouldn't even have been as close as it was. Eighteen months later, he had the last laugh, taking twenty-three wickets as the Ashes urn was regained in the most emphatic manner possible.

As arguably the finest captain Australia never had, his tactical awareness and strategic genius was instrumental in the Rajasthan Royals winning the inaugural Indian Premier League in 2008.

Muttiah Muralitharan   international career 1992–2011

'To Benjamin Franklin's assertion that death and taxes are the only certainties can now be added the eternal nature of Murali's 800.' Mike Selvey

Few cricketers have polarised opinion quite as much as Muttiah Muralitharan. Never mind the fact that he retired as the leading wicket-taker in both Test and ODI cricket, the man known universally as 'Murali' had to face constant scrutiny over his action. However, once it had been cleared, he evolved into the most prolific wicket-taker in international cricket history.

Player	Team	Wickets
M. Muralitharan	**SL**	**1,347**
S.K. Warne	Aus	**1,001**
A. Kumble	Ind	**956**
G.D. McGrath	Aus	**949**
Wasim Akram	Pak	**916**

He was a true innovator – a wrist-spinner who bowled off breaks, but when he returned home from touring England with Sri Lanka in 1991 without a wicket to his name, he might have been tempted to give it all up and return to the role he played for his school as a middle-order batsman.

His international career began relatively slowly, with no hint of the world records to follow. However, a combination of flexible wrists, deformed elbow and fast shoulder rotation soon made him unplayable – especially in helpful conditions to spin bowling. His sixteen wickets at The Oval in 1998 made a mockery of the fact that Sri Lanka were only afforded one end-of-season Test in England and matters were put right when they next toured.

That performance marked his transformation from a good into a great bowler. Once he mastered the doosra, he became a true master, able to run through any side on any surface. It took him twenty-seven Test matches to take 100 Test wickets, but from then on, the landmarks came thick and fast. His next seven blocks of a hundred wickets came in just 15, 16, 14, 15, 14, 12 and, finally, 20 matches, when he was starting to feel the effects of having bowled more deliveries than anyone else.

It was on tours of Australia that most controversy reared its head. Repeatedly no-balled for throwing by Darrell Hair and Ross Emerson, it was due to exhaustive analysis of his bowling action that 15 degrees of tolerance was brought in when analysing actions, thereby changing the face of the world bowling scene forever.

He ended his Test career – fittingly – with a wicket from his final delivery making him the only player to take 800 wickets in that form of the game. Similarly, his number of five-wicket and ten-wicket hauls are records that are unlikely to ever be broken.

Player	Team	5wl	Player	Team	10wM
M. Muralitharan	SL	67	M. Muralitharan	SL	22
S.K. Warne	Aus	37	S.K. Warne	Aus	10
R.J. Hadlee	NZ	36	R.J. Hadlee	NZ	9
A. Kumble	Ind	35	H.M.R.K.B. Herath	SL	9
H.M.R.K.B. Herath	SL	34	A. Kumble	Ind	8

Russel Arnold dropped a catch at short leg against Zimbabwe at Kandy in 2002 which would have given him all ten wickets in an innings, but he could still content himself with joining Jim Laker as the only two bowlers to twice take at least nine wickets in a Test innings.

His ding-dong battle with Shane Warne for supremacy as leading Test spinner enthralled audiences for the best part of a decade and a half. Shoulder surgery slowed Murali's progress, but his dismissal of Paul Collingwood at Kandy in December 2007 took him to 709 and he was out in front for good.

For Murali it was always about more than the wickets. For a country torn apart by civil war, he became its leading light, helping to inspire his team to World Cup glory in 1996.

Hedley Verity   international career 1931–39

'He was a born schemer; tireless, but never wild, in experiment; as sensitive in observation as a good host, or as an instrumentalist who spots a rival on the beat; the scholar who does not only dream, the inventor who can make it work.' R.C. Robertson-Glasgow

It is the bowling equivalent of Brian Lara's 501 not out – Hedley Verity's remarkable figures of ten wickets for 10 runs for Yorkshire against Nottinghamshire at Leeds in 1932 – that remain the best bowling figures in first-class cricket.

Player	Figures	Match	Venue	Year
H. Verity	**10-10**	**Yorkshire v Nottinghamshire**	**Leeds**	**1932**
G. Geary	**10-18**	Leicestershire v Glamorgan	Pontypridd	1929
P.M. Chatterjee	**10-20**	Bengal v Assam	Jorhat	1957
A.E.E. Vogler	**10-26**	E Province v Griqualand West	Johannesburg	1906
A.E. Moss	**10-28**	Canterbury v Wellington	Christchurch	1889
W.P. Howell	**10-28**	Australians v Surrey	The Oval	1899
Naeem Akhtar	**10-28**	Rawalpindi Blues v Peshawar	Peshawar	1995

When he performed that feat, he was 28 years old and still to emerge fully from the shadow of the great Wilfred Rhodes, who personified Yorkshire cricket for more than three decades. Despite having been born a stone's throw from Yorkshire's home ground of Headingley, Verity had to be content playing league cricket until he was 25, spending time with Rawdon, Accrington and Middleton.

Rhodes' view of his slow left-arm successor was a simple 'He'll do'. And how he did! He ended his first-class career with 1,956 wickets at just 14.90 apiece, of which fifteen came in the 1934 Lord's Test, which proved to be England's last victory over Australia on the ground until 2009. His performance was so great it even warranted a mention by Hercule Poirot in *Four and Twenty Blackbirds*.

Bowling at almost a slow-medium pace, his greatest strength was unnerving accuracy, with an ability to adjust his flight depending on how much assistance he received from the conditions. He was especially effective at running through the latter-order batsmen, often sending them on their way with a succession of inswinging yorkers.

His first major contribution in Test cricket was overshadowed by the controversy of the 'Bodyline' series in Australia in the winter of 1932/33, but in the final Test at Sydney, he took eight wickets to hasten England to an eight-wicket victory. The following summer he took seventeen Essex wickets in a single day, just the second of three bowlers to perform the feat.

Player	Figures	Match	Venue	Year
C. Blythe	17-48	Kent v Northamptonshire	Northampton	1907
H. Verity	**17-91**	**Yorkshire v Essex**	**Leyton**	**1933**
T.W.J. Goddard	17-106	Gloucestershire v Kent	Bristol	1939

In a period characterised by timeless Test matches, blameless pitches and mountains of runs, Verity's Test record of 144 wickets at just 24 runs apiece was particularly remarkable. As was his record against Donald Bradman, whom he dismissed eight times in Tests – more than any other bowler – while conceding just 398 runs. Therefore, the Don's average against Verity was 49.75, almost exactly half his career average of 99.94.

He took a career-best 211 wickets in 1935 as Yorkshire won the championship but he couldn't pick up wickets consistently against the touring South Africans. He even struggled in Yorkshire's match against the tourists, Jock Cameron striking him for 30 runs in one over, prompting wicketkeeper Arthur Wood to remark that Verity had him in two minds – not knowing whether to hit him for four or six!

On 1 September 1939, as war threatened to engulf Europe, he took seven Sussex wickets for just 9 runs and as he walked off, he wondered if he would ever bowl at Hove again.

Alas, he was to be proved right. The rest of the season was cancelled and he became a company commander, eventually being posted to Italy. In July 1943, he was hit in the chest and died a prisoner of war – the second great England left-arm spinner to lose his life on the battlefield following Colin Blythe twenty-six years earlier.

Clarrie Grimmett   international career 1925–36

'So great was his own love for the game that, at 70, he still had an occasional bowl in his garden, but was heard to say that he had lost some of his pace from the pitch.' Ian Peebles

Australian great Clarrie Grimmett was born in New Zealand, where he attended Mount Cook Boys' School in Wellington. While he was there, he came under the mindful eye of Mr Hempelman, who convinced him to give up pace bowling and turn to spin instead. Once the First World War had broken out, he moved to Australia, primarily to further his career as a signwriter, but it took a full five years for him to break into the Victoria team.

It was a move to South Australia in 1924 that saw an immediate upturn in his fortunes and he made his Test debut at the age of 33, making up for lost time by taking eleven inexpensive wickets against England at Sydney, his balding head concealed by a cap as he twirled over after over.

Grimmett is credited for inventing the 'flipper', which is squeezed out of the front of the hand and has been the staple diet of leg-break bowlers ever since. His partnership with fellow leggie Bill O'Reilly flourished in part due to O'Reilly's unusual preference to bowl downwind so that Grimmett could have the other end.

He was one of the first slow bowlers to prove that a leg-spinner was not just a luxury, but such a bowler could be both effective and economical. He conceded runs at just 2.16 per over – remarkable enough for a leg-spinner – but he had to contend with the likes of Hobbs, Hammond and Sutcliffe in the opposition ranks.

Despite frequently taking only ninety seconds to complete an over, he delivered just a solitary no-ball in the entire course of his career and often irked the other bowlers, who were not able to rest for long enough between their overs. He ended his career with thirteen wickets in his final Test at Durban at the age of 44 and the then Test record of 216 wickets at nearly six per match. Of all the bowlers to have taken at least 200 Test wickets, only one has taken more wickets per Test.

Player	Team	Matches	Wickets	W/M
M. Muralitharan	SL	133	800	**6.02**
C.V. Grimmett	**Aus**	**37**	**216**	**5.84**
Yasir Shah	Pak	42	224	**5.33**
R. Ashwin	Ind	70	362	**5.17**
D.K. Lillee	Aus	70	355	**5.07**
R.J. Hadlee	NZ	86	431	**5.01**

No one escaped his wiles, especially not the more inexperienced West Indians and South Africans, against whom he took 110 wickets in just fifteen matches. He also contributed greatly to Australia's Ashes successes in England in the 1930s, taking twenty-nine wickets in 1930 and twenty-five more four years later. When he was overlooked for the 1938 tour – on account of his age – Bill Ponsford described the decision as 'sheer lunacy'.

He continued to take wickets by the bucketload in domestic cricket, and his final record tally of Sheffield Shield wickets is unlikely to ever be broken.

Player	Matches	Wickets
C.V. Grimmett	79	513
M.S. Kasprowicz	101	441
A.J. Bichel	89	430
J. Angel	105	419
T.M. Alderman	97	384

By the time he finally retired at the age of 49, he could have put his signwriting skills to good effect on the honours boards at cricket grounds around the world.

Jim Laker   international career 1948–59

'When you batted against Jim Laker you could hear the ball fizz as he spun it.'
Garry Sobers

Even if he had never taken another wicket in his career, Jim Laker's name would live forever as a result of his feats in the 1956 Old Trafford Ashes Test. No one has even taken eighteen wickets in a first-class match in the last 150 years, so Laker's was the bowling equivalent of Bob Beamon's leap in 1968, which bypassed 28 feet to become the first 29-foot long jump in history.

Bowling	Player	Team	Against	Venue	Year
19-90	**J.C. Laker**	**England**	**Australia**	**Manchester**	**1956**
17-48	C. Blythe	Kent	Northamptonshire	Northampton	1907
17-50	C.T.B. Turner	Australians	England XI	Hastings	1888

What is even more remarkable is that none of the other spinners in the match had much success – his partner in crime for so many triumphs, Tony Lock, ending with match figures of one wicket for 106 runs.

Perhaps Laker's 1956 achievements should not have come as such a surprise. Earlier that same season he had taken all ten Australian wickets for 88 when playing for Surrey, and his love affair with Australian batsmen had started way back in the 1940s. He joined the Royal Army Ordnance Corps during the war, and as a corporal serving in Egypt, he had taken six wickets for just 10 runs against the Australian servicemen.

His early love of cricket was encouraged by his aunt, and he started his career as a middle-order batsman and fast bowler. In one game for Salts High School, he took six wickets for no runs as they dismissed their opposition for just one run. Having left school, he attended Herbert Sutcliffe's Indoor School, based at Headingley, and it was there – on the suggestion of former Yorkshire opening batsman B.B. Wilson – that he started to bowl off spin.

When he returned from his overseas service, he was posted to Catford, in South-East London, and earned a trial with Surrey. Surprisingly, Yorkshire obliged, and so Laker moved south to ply his trade at The Oval. He topped the Surrey bowling averages in 1947 and earned a call-up to England's tour of the Caribbean that winter.

Making his Test debut at Bridgetown, he took 7-103 in the West Indies first innings, ending with a spell of six wickets for 25 runs. The following summer saw Australia conquer all, but it could have been a very different story at Leeds had England taken one of the three chances Bradman offered on his way to an unbeaten 173. As it was, none were taken, and Australia scored 404-3 on the final day to win.

In 1950, he monopolised the traditional 'Test Trial' match at his hometown of Bradford, which pitted the England team against what amounted to an England Second XI. Coming on after just twelve overs, he immediately found his length and turned the ball incredibly, ending with the remarkable figures of eight wickets for 2 runs, which remains the cheapest eight-wicket haul in history.

Bowling	Player	Match	Venue	Year
8-2	**J.C. Laker**	**England v The Rest**	**Bradford**	**1950**
8-4	D. Shackleton	Hampshire v Somerset	Weston-super-Mare	1955
8-5	E. Peate	Yorkshire v Surrey	Holbeck	1883
8-7	J. Bickley	England v Kent and Sussex	Lord's	1856
8-7	G.A. Lohmann	England v South Africa	Port Elizabeth	1896
8-7	C.H. Palmer	Leicestershire v Surrey	Leicester	1955

Despite his success in the trial, he only played one Test that summer, and only toured once with England in the next six years.

He ended with a total of 193 Test wickets at an average of 21.24 in his forty-six Tests, despite missing fifty-three more Tests over the course of his career. To this date, no one has taken more Test wickets for England at a better average.

For those too young to remember his great performances on the field, they could gain comfort in the fact that he subsequently became an outspoken but much-respected commentator.

Colin Blythe   international career 1901–10

'The best left-hander on English wickets I have ever seen. His remarkable flighting of the ball and his deception in pace are the best I ever met.' Charles Macartney

The 'Golden Age' of cricket is nostalgically thought of more as a golden age of batsmen rather than bowlers. However, in Albert Chevallier Tayler's famous painting depicting Kent v Lancashire at Canterbury in 1906, the focus is not on the batsman, but on Colin Blythe bowling from the Pavilion End, with the flags fluttering behind him.

Without doubt the greatest player to be killed in the First World War, the conflict ended his first-class career at the age of 35, and he played his last Test at just 32. Despite his fragile build and suffering from epilepsy, he still managed to craft one of the greatest of all cricket careers.

Born in Deptford, the eldest of thirteen children, he was a competent violinist and learned his cricket on the vast expanse of Blackheath, on which there could be up to twenty matches running concurrently. His father worked as an engine fitter at Woolwich Arsenal, but Blythe managed to avoid following in his father's footsteps by a stroke of luck when he was attending a match between Kent and Somerset at Rectory Field, Blackheath, in 1897.

Kent's Walter Wright came out to practise and invited the 18-year-old Blythe to bowl to him. Looking on was the manager of the Tonbridge Cricket Nursery, who was impressed and invited the youngster to a trial at the county ground. A month later, he was on the staff, while still working alongside his father in the winter months.

Possessing a remarkable combination of flight and spin, he was simply unplayable on wickets that offered even a hint of assistance. Never afraid to be driven, he would counter-attack with even more inviting flight and greater spin. His quicker ball was more of a medium-pace inswinger, which yorked many an unsuspecting batsman.

His total of 2,503 first-class wickets stands thirteenth on that particular list, and his career had many highlights. Perhaps his greatest achievement was his haul of fifteen South African wickets at Leeds in 1907 to bring England victory in a Test in which they had been bowled out for 76 in the first innings of the match. They are still the best figures by an England bowler against South Africa in England.

Bowling	Player	Venue	Year
15-99	**C. Blythe**	**Leeds**	**1907**
13-57	S.F. Barnes	The Oval	1912
12-101	R. Tattersall	Lord's	1951
12-112	A.V. Bedser	Manchester	1951
12-171	A.P. Freeman	Manchester	1929

His eleven wickets earned England an Ashes victory at Edgbaston in 1909, and he signed off from Test cricket with ten wickets at Cape Town in March 1910. But it was Northamptonshire, on 1 June 1907, who were singled out for a truly record-breaking feat.

Replying to Kent's first-innings total of 254, Northants were soon in trouble, collapsing to 4 runs for seven wickets, all seven of which fell to Blythe in six overs at a personal cost of just a single. The tail wagged, but Blythe polished off the innings to finish with 10-30, and the follow-on was enforced with Kent leading by 194.

He wasn't finished there, taking 7-18 in the second innings as Northants were dismissed for just 39. Blythe's match figures of 17-48 remain a County Championship record, more than a hundred years later.

Bowling	Player	Match	Venue	Year
17-48	**C. Blythe**	**Kent v Northamptonshire**	**Northampton**	**1907**
17-56	C.L. Parker	Gloucestershire v Essex	Gloucester	1925
17-67	A.P. Freeman	Kent v Sussex	Hove	1922
17-86	K.J. Abbott	Hampshire v Somerset	Southampton	2019
17-89	W.G. Grace	Gloucestershire v Nottinghamshire	Cheltenham	1877
17-89	F. Matthews	Nottinghamshire v Northamptonshire	Nottingham	1923

In late 1917, while serving with the 12th Battalion of the King's Own Yorkshire Light Infantry, Blythe went out to face the horrors of the Battle of Passchendaele as an engineer working on a military railway line. On the evening of 8 November, a German shrapnel shell burst behind the enemy line. Five men were killed, one of whom was Blythe.

Bill O'Reilly   international career 1932–46

'Off the field, he could be your lifelong buddy, but out in the middle, he had all the lovable qualities of a demented rhinoceros.' Colin McCool

The greatest bowler of his time, in the opinion of Don Bradman, Bill O'Reilly played only club cricket until he was 18. He moved up to grade cricket in 1926, and played three first-class matches the following year before fading into obscurity for four more years. However, he then came back and found himself in the Test side within six weeks. In his second Test, played at Melbourne, he helped bowl South Africa out for just 36 and 45, and for the rest of the 1930s he was a virtual ever-present in the Australian team in an era characterised by timeless Tests and shirtfront pitches.

He first encountered Bradman in January 1925, when he was an undergraduate at Sydney University's Teacher Training College. Dragged off the train at the town of Bowral on his journey home to Wingello, he was asked to represent his local side, who were at the Glebe Oval to play Bowral, for whom a young boy who was 'bloody good' was playing.

At the end of the day's play, Bradman was undefeated on 234 in 165 minutes, but when the match resumed the following week at the Wingello Recreation Ground, O'Reilly's first delivery pitched just outside leg stump and bowled him around his legs.

Australia were defeated in the 1932/33 'Bodyline' series, but O'Reilly took twenty-seven wickets in the five Tests, and he helped New South Wales to win the Sheffield Shield the same season with thirty-one wickets. On the 1934 Ashes tour he took eleven wickets in the Trent Bridge win, and as England piled up 627 in their first innings at Manchester, he dismissed Walters, captain Wyatt and Hammond in the space of one over on his way to figures of 7-189 in fifty-nine overs. Bizarrely, in four of the Tests of that 1934 series, Australia fielded five players with the first name William: Bill Ponsford, Bill Woodfull, Bill Brown, Bill O'Reilly and William 'Bert' Oldfield.

O'Reilly formed a formidable spin pairing with Clarrie Grimmett; in the fifteen matches they played together they totalled 169 wickets between them – eighty-eight for Grimmett and eighty-one for O'Reilly. And the two of them were among the top three wicket-takers in Test cricket in the 1930s.

Player	Team	Matches	**Wickets**
C.V. Grimmett	Aus	28	**169**
H. Verity	Eng	40	**144**
W.J. O'Reilly	**Aus**	**26**	136
W. Voce	Eng	24	**97**

Unlike the diminutive Grimmett, O'Reilly was tall – standing 6 feet 2 inches, and his key strength was the ability to vary his pace and flight without any discernible change in his action. His large hands enabled him to turn the ball either way, and he was always a threat to the batsman on both edges of the bat. Fast for a spinner, he operated at almost medium pace and possessed a temperament far more suited to pace bowling. At domestic level, he was phenomenal, ending his career with the best average among all the bowlers to have taken at least 100 wickets in the Sheffield Shield.

Player	Team	Matches	Wickets	**Avge**
W.J. O'Reilly	**NSW**	**33**	203	**17.10**
G. Noblet	SA	38	190	**17.87**
T.R. McKibbin	NSW	18	137	**20.83**
H. Trumble	Vic	30	159	**20.92**
A.K. Davidson	NSW	62	246	**21.11**

Having retired at the end of the 1934 tour to concentrate on teaching, a job at Sydney Grammar School enabled him to continue his cricket career and he played a key role in Australia's memorable 1936/37 Ashes triumph when they came back from 0-2 down to win the series 3-2. O'Reilly's contribution was twenty-five wickets in the series, including eight in the deciding fifth Test at Melbourne.

In his only post-war Test, he took 5-14 and 3-19 as a poor New Zealand team were dismissed for 42 and 54 at Wellington and Australia's total of 199-8 declared was easily enough to give an innings victory. At the end of the match, he hurled his boots out of the dressing room window to signal that this time his retirement would be for good.

Anil Kumble   international career 1990–2008

India has produced many great spinners, but when all the wickets are added up, none of them come close to Anil Kumble, who retired as India's greatest-ever Test wicket-taker – fast or slow.

Player	Matches	Wickets	Avge
A. Kumble	**132**	**619**	**29.65**
Kapil Dev	131	**434**	29.64
Harbhajan Singh	103	**417**	32.46
R. Ashwin	70	**362**	25.36
Z. Khan	92	**311**	32.94

Eschewing the traditional 'loop' of a leg-spinner for a faster, flatter trajectory, he perfected his art on the matting wickets of his club cricket in Bangalore, which were laid out on top of baked mud. He made the most of his height, delivering the ball from as high as he possibly could, to maximise the bounce. Relatively few of his victims were stumped, as batsmen preferred to play him from the relative safety of the crease, but they were often bamboozled by his impeccable line or by a ball that skidded through to either hit the stumps or trap them lbw.

He graduated with a Bachelor's degree in Mechanical Engineering from Rashtreeya Vidyalaya College and soon afterwards made his Test debut at Old Trafford as part of a twin leg-spinning attack with Narendra Hirwani. However, it was somewhat of a difficult start as England's Graham Gooch and Mike Atherton piled on 225 for the first wicket, and the bespectacled Kumble was discarded from the Test side for two years.

Once he was recalled, he quickly made up for lost time, racing to 100 Test wickets in just twenty-one Tests. He was one of the leading figures in England's 'spinwash' tour in 1993, taking twenty-one wickets and his figures of 6-12 against the West Indies the same year remained an Indian ODI record for twenty-one years.

He enjoyed a sensational summer with Northamptonshire in the County Championship in 1995, becoming the first leg-spinner for nearly a quarter of a century to pass a hundred wickets in a season. He bowled the county to some extraordinary victories, not least when they won by an innings after conceding 527 against Nottinghamshire.

However, without doubt his greatest feat came at Delhi in 1999, when he took all ten Pakistan wickets at a cost of 74 runs to become just the second man to take ten wickets in a Test innings. That performance led India to its first Test victory over Pakistan for nineteen years.

By that time, he was expected to run through opposing batsmen in India, but he was also able to conjure Test victories for them abroad. He took seven wickets in the match at the traditional seamer's paradise of Headingley in 2002, and first-innings figures of 5-154 brought victory at Adelaide the following year. He subsequently took twelve wickets in the 2004 New Year's Day Test at Sydney, but Steve Waugh stood firm to thwart him at the death. He was instrumental in orchestrating India's first-ever series victory in Pakistan, with 6-72 at Multan and 4-47 at Rawalpindi in 2004, and their first in the Caribbean for thirty-five years in 2006.

His other major career highlight came at The Oval in 2007, when – in his 118th Test – he finally scored his first Test century, by far the longest anyone has ever had to wait to achieve such a landmark.

Player	Team	Matches
A. Kumble	**Ind**	**118**
W.P.U.J.C. Vaas	SL	**97**
Harbhajan Singh	Ind	**88**
J.N. Gillespie	Aus	**71**
H.H. Streak	Zim	**56**

Few players have been so highly respected among their peers. Post-retirement, he served as president of the Karnataka State Cricket Association, chairman of the National Cricket Academy, and in October 2012 he was appointed as the chairman of the ICC Cricket Committee.

Derek Underwood   **international career 1966–82**

'The face of a choirboy, the demeanour of a civil servant and the ruthlessness of a rat-catcher.' Geoff Boycott

Derek Underwood was unusual among the spinners of his time, as he possessed a long run-up and bowled at a faster pace. At school he hoped to be a fast bowler but found that when he moved from youth to adult cricket, he wasn't quick anymore and so had to adapt to different circumstances.

On pitches that offered some spin, he was not afraid to give the ball a rip, but it was his uncanny accuracy and immaculate length that caused frustration among batsmen. His arm-ball was a full inswinger and he formed an almost telepathic connection with wicketkeeper Alan Knott, who was so often his co-conspirator in many dismissals for both Kent and England.

His father was a useful seamer who played for Farnborough and he was so keen to encourage his two sons that he constructed a net in their back garden, complete with a concrete pitch topped with matting. On the recommendation of fellow left-armer Tony Lock, Derek was given a trial at Kent, and by 1963 he was in the first team, at the tender age of 17.

By the end of his first season he had taken 101 first-class wickets, becoming the youngest ever bowler to pass the three-figure mark. For good measure, he repeated the feat the following year, before claiming 157 scalps in 1966, and was the first Kent bowler to top the national averages since Colin Blythe in 1914.

27 August 1968 was the date that sealed Derek Underwood's reputation as one of the greatest cricketers of his era. Rain had flooded The Oval and England captain Colin Cowdrey implored the groundsmen to somehow get the outfield dry. At 2.15 pm, he used the ground PA system to beg assistance from the crowd and incredibly, at 4.45, play restarted, with England having seventy-five minutes to take the remaining five Australian wickets.

Almost as a last throw of the dice, the unlikely Basil D'Oliveira made the breakthrough, and then it was down to Underwood. He took the last four wickets for 6 runs in twenty-seven deliveries as England sealed victory with John Inverarity padding up to an arm-ball with just six minutes remaining.

If that was the defining moment of his career, there were plenty that ran it close. He reached 1,000 first-class wickets at the age of just 25 and ended with a total of 2,465 in all first-class cricket. In 1974, he took 13-71 in the match against Pakistan at Lord's, and ended his Test career with 297 wickets – the most by any England spinner.

Player	Matches	Wickets
D.L. Underwood	86	**297**
G.P. Swann	60	**255**
J.C. Laker	46	**193**
M.M. Ali	60	**181**
G.A.R. Lock	49	**174**

His haul could have been even greater, but he joined World Series Cricket in 1977 and toured South Africa with Graham Gooch's team in 1982, thereby depriving himself of more possible Test victims.

However, the achievement that probably gave him the most joy was his only first-class century, which came against Sussex at Hastings in 1984. He had come in as nightwatchman on the Saturday evening, took 6-12 in the Sunday League game the following day, and continued his innings to three figures on the Monday. It was the same ground on which he had recorded his career-best bowling figures – of 9-28, back in 1964. Coming in his 591st match, it was the longest anyone has ever waited before reaching three figures for the first time.

Player	Matches
D.L. Underwood	**591**
R.W. Taylor	**539**
F.S. Trueman	**418**
G.S. Boyes	**413**
W. Attewell	**374**

Bishan Bedi   **international career 1966–79**

'When Bishan Bedi bowled, every day seemed bathed in sunshine.' Pat Murphy

When asked to describe his idea of heaven, Jim Laker – no mean judge of a bowler – replied that it would have Ray Lindwall bowling from one end and Bishan Bedi from the other. Bedi was the perfect fusion of courtesy and fierce competition, all wrapped up in one of the most beautiful bowling actions of all time.

Born in the Sikh capital of Amritsar, he strengthened his spinning fingers by playing marbles as a youth, and his brightly coloured turbans and youthful exuberance were to become as much of his trademark as the mesmerising spells he bowled throughout his career. He was playing first-class cricket for Northern Punjab at the age of 15, and India came beckoning when he had just turned 20 years old.

It was a magical time for Indian spin, with Chandrasekhar, Prasanna and Venkat joined by the new left-arm spinner. In fact, they only all took the field together once, as usually one of the off-spinners was left out. That was at Edgbaston in 1967, which ended in a 132-run defeat, but it was the Indian batting that failed on that occasion.

Bedi helped script a memorable series victory in New Zealand in early 1968, taking fourteen wickets on the traditionally spin-unfriendly pitches, and followed up with fifteen more when New Zealand paid a return visit to India the following year. He became a star in the follow-up series against Bill Lawry's Australians when he took a total of twenty-one wickets in the five Tests, including nine wickets at Delhi and a career-best 7-98 at Kolkata.

He took twenty-five wickets in each of the 1972/73 and 1976/77 England tours to his country and enjoyed a prolific six-season spell with Northamptonshire in the mid-1970s. His love of bowling in English conditions was emphasised with his spell against East Africa in the 1975 World Cup, which remains the most economical in the tournament's history.

RPO	Bowling	Player	Team	Against	Venue	Year
0.50	**12-8-6-1**	**B.S. Bedi**	**India**	**East Africa**	**Leeds**	**1975**
0.80	10-5-8-4	C.M. Old	England	Canada	Manchester	1979
0.80	10-4-8-2	C.E.L. Ambrose	West Indies	Scotland	Leicester	1999
0.83	12-6-10-0	R.J. Hadlee	New Zealand	East Africa	Birmingham	1975
0.91	12-6-11-4	J.A. Snow	England	East Africa	Birmingham	1975
0.91	12-5-11-2	D.S. de Silva	Sri Lanka	New Zealand	Derby	1983

He was elevated to the Indian captaincy in early 1976, but it was a reign marked by controversy. He helped oversee a memorable win at Port of Spain in which India had scored a world-record 406 to beat the West Indies, but his tactics in the following match at Kingston were baffling. He opted to declare India's second innings closed with five wickets in hand, and still behind in the match in protest of what he considered sustained intimidatory bowling by the hosts.

India performed well on the following year's tour to Australia and levelled the five-match series with just the final match to play, but lost the decider at Melbourne. However, it was defeat in Pakistan that spelled the end of his time in charge, not helped by forfeiting a One Day International at Sahiwal, when he called his batsmen in when on the verge of victory after Sarfraz Nawaz had bowled four successive bouncers. Soon afterwards, fellow left-arm spinner Dilip Doshi took eight wickets on his Test debut against Australia, and that effectively ended Bedi's Test career. However, that was not before he had taken more first-class wickets than any other Indian in history.

Player	Matches	Wickets	Avge
B.S. Bedi	370	1,560	21.69
S. Venkataraghavan	341	1,390	24.14
A. Kumble	244	1,136	25.83
B.S. Chandrasekhar	246	1,063	24.03

In retirement, he was never afraid to court controversy, with outspoken views on everything from Murali's action to Twenty20 cricket. However, he was always delighted to offer advice to any young spinner keen to make their way in the game.

Lance Gibbs   international career 1958–76

'Bulbous but dreamy eyes, close cropped hair and the loosest of gaits gave Gibbs the appearance of a New Orleans trombonist.' David Frith

Ironically, the first West Indian to hold the world Test wicket-taking record was not one of their famed speed merchants, but rather a tall off-spinner who bounced his way to the wicket. More than sixty years after his debut, Lance Gibbs is still the leading West Indian spinner by a country mile.

Player	Matches	Wickets	Avge
L.R. Gibbs	**79**	**309**	**29.09**
S. Ramadhin	43	**158**	28.98
A.L. Valentine	36	**139**	30.32
D. Bishoo	36	**117**	37.17
C.L. Hooper	102	**114**	49.42

Gibbs was ten years older than his cousin Clive Lloyd and he started his career bowling leg breaks at Demerara Cricket Club, which was later to produce Roy Fredericks and Roger Harper. It was only after advice from former England wicketkeeper Arthur McIntyre that he concentrated on turning the ball from off to leg.

His first-class debut came at the age of 19 for British Guiana against the touring MCC, and he made his first two wickets memorable. First to fall was Denis Compton, bowled for 18, and his next victim was Tom Graveney – but not after he had shared a fourth wicket stand of 402 with Len Hutton. However, Gibbs could always look back safe in the knowledge that his first two victims ended their first-class careers with 245 centuries between them.

When his Test debut came four years later, it was just his sixth first-class match, and he played four Tests in the high-scoring 1957/58 series with Pakistan, taking seventeen wickets, and soon usurped Ramadhin and Valentine as the first-choice spinner.

He wasn't selected for the famous Brisbane tied Test in 1960, but made up for it three Tests later at Adelaide when he became just the second West Indian bowler to take a Test hat-trick. From then on, he dominated the decade, regularly bowling the West Indies to victory, most memorably with a spell of eight wickets for 6 runs in 15.3 overs against India at Barbados in 1962.

He found Australia to his liking again at Georgetown in 1965, when he took 6-29 in their first innings, and he inspired an innings victory over England at Old Trafford the following year with five wickets in each innings. Another away innings victory came at Kolkata in early 1967, when he managed to out-bowl the home spinners Venkat, Bedi and Chandrasekhar.

At the end of the decade, a dip in form caused him to be left out of the team for 34-year-old Jack Noreiga, who promptly took 9-95 against India at Port of Spain. But it was for Warwickshire that he recaptured his form in spectacular style in the summer of 1971, taking 131 first-class wickets in twenty-six matches to propel himself back into the international reckoning.

His final great performances on the international stage came under the captaincy of his cousin Lloyd in India in early 1975, when he took 6-76 at Delhi and helped seal the series win by taking 7-98 in India's first innings in the deciding Test at Mumbai.

The 1975/76 tour of Australia was a difficult one for the West Indies, but there was the crumb of comfort of Gibbs overtaking Fred Trueman's world record of 307 Test wickets when he dismissed Ian Redpath at Melbourne. His world record may now be long gone, but he remains the bowler to have bowled the most Test deliveries while conceding fewer than 2 runs per over during an entire career.

Player	Team	Balls	Economy
L.R. Gibbs	**WI**	**27,115**	**1.98**
F.J. Titmus	Eng	**15,118**	1.95
S. Ramadhin	WI	**13,939**	1.97
H.J. Tayfield	SA	**13,568**	1.94
A.L. Valentine	WI	**12,953**	1.95

Saqlain Mushtaq   international career 1995–2004

'County batsmen in the first few years came out to bat with fear in their eyes. Not wanting to look stupid, basically!' Ian Ward

Towards the end of the twentieth century, the name of Saqlain Mushtaq was added to the names Bosanquet and Grimmett in terms of innovation with the ball. His introduction of the doosra – a delivery that was bowled with the same action as a traditional off-spinner but spun the other way – added a new weapon to a spinner's arsenal, in the way Bosanquet's googly and Grimmett's flipper had decades earlier.

Unlike others who turned to spin after early experimentation with pace bowling, off breaks were always Saqlain's first love. He spent many hours playing street cricket with his two brothers in Lahore using a tennis ball bound with electrical tape, which enabled him to perfect the art of the delivery that went the other way. After three years of cricket at college, he was picked to make his first-class debut, and a Test debut came a year later at the age of just 18.

If he was a steady performer in Test cricket, it was his performances in One Day International cricket that attracted most attention. In his first full year in the team, he established a record for the most ODI wickets in a calendar year, and then did even better the following year, setting a mark that still stands.

Player	Year	Team	Matches	Wickets
Saqlain Mushtaq	**1997**	**Pak**	36	69
Saqlain Mushtaq	**1996**	**Pak**	33	65
S.K. Warne	1999	Aus	37	62
Saeed Ajmal	2013	Pak	33	62
A. Kumble	1996	Ind	32	61
S.M. Pollock	2000	SA	38	61
Abdul Razzaq	2000	Pak	38	61

His impact was so great that he became the fastest bowler in history in terms of time to reach the landmark of 100 ODI wickets, and to this day, no one else has got there in less than two years.

Time	Player	Team	Matches
1y 225d	**Saqlain Mushtaq**	**Pak**	**53**
2y 100d	I.K. Pathan	Ind	59
2y 158d	Rashid Khan	Afg	43
2y 162d	Z. Khan	Ind	65
2y 208d	K. Yadav	Ind	58
2y 251d	A.B. Agarkar	Ind	67

He took two hat-tricks in ODI cricket and became the first player from Pakistan to perform the feat in the World Cup when he dismissed three Zimbabweans in a row at The Oval in 1999. All the while, his superb control enabled him to become one of the first spin bowlers to specialise in bowling the closing overs of a one-day innings.

For all his successes in the shorter form of the game, arguably his greatest moment came in Test cricket. His five wickets in each innings at Chennai in early 1999 overcame a century by a half-fit Sachin Tendulkar and clinched a nail-biting 12-run victory for Pakistan. Twenty years later, Pakistani cricket fans overwhelmingly voted that performance as the greatest Test win in their country's history.

He followed up with ten more wickets in the next match, but that effort was overshadowed by Anil Kumble's ten wickets in an innings, levelling the series. However, the series was clinched for Pakistan in the final Test at Kolkata, enabling them to record just their second series win in India.

He played ten seasons for Surrey, and never was he better than in his earlier days, when he bowled them to the County Championship title in 1999, 2000 and 2002. His first thirty-nine first-class matches for the county brought a scarcely believable 219 wickets at an average of just 15.57 apiece.

His international career was over before he turned 30, as other bowlers had started to master the doosra and Shoaib Malik's greater batting prowess took his ODI slot, while Danish Kaneria was preferred in the longer format. However, to this day, his contribution to spin bowling still marks him as a true innovator.

Afterword

One of the fascinating things about lists is that virtually everyone has one. Restrict that to cricket and everyone will have several, and no one will agree on everything. They won't even necessarily agree on who should be number one, so heaven help them if they try to agree on numbers one through ninety-nine.

You must be a reasonable player to represent your country at that level – with the possible exception of the early South African teams who were roundly humiliated by Johnny Briggs, John Ferris and George Lohmann respectively in the 1888/89, 1891/92 and 1895/96 series.

The players in this book really are the greatest of the great. More than 3,000 men have played Test cricket since the first match in 1877, and this list was compiled backwards. Rather than start with player number one and moving on, the list was whittled down from 3,000 to 1,000, to 500 to 150, and then to the final tally here.

This book contains fewer than 4 per cent of all Test Cricketers, so there is certainly no disgrace being on the outside. Reducing anything to a smaller list is fraught with controversy and I agonised long and hard over most of these players. Here is a top-class side of players who missed out:

Bert Sutcliffe: two first-class triple centuries, his innings of 385 was the highest by a leftie until 1994
Tom Hayward: the second batsman to hit a hundred first-class centuries
Phil Mead: scored the most runs in County Championship history
Vijay Merchant: averaged 71 in first-class cricket
Ted Dexter: retired at 33 and went on to invent the ICC World Rankings
George Hirst: performed the 'double double' – 2,385 runs and 208 wickets in a single season
Brendon McCullum: the first New Zealander to score a Test triple-century
Richie Benaud: the first player to complete the 2,000 run/200 wicket double in Test cricket
Alan Davidson: the first to score 100 runs and take ten wickets in the same Test
Joel Garner: took three five-wicket hauls in Lord's finals
Lasith Malinga: the first bowler twice to take four wickets in four balls in international cricket

However, including all of them would have made the total 110, and might have tempted me to open the floodgates.

I am not sure if anyone can truthfully admit who the greatest players of all time actually were. Even if most aficionados pick Don Bradman as their top batsman, how would he have fared against the West Indian pace attack of the 1970s and 1980s, and what would his record have been had the Second World War not interrupted Test cricket for nearly seven years? Was Len Hutton better than Graham Gooch? Could Virat Kohli have scored runs on uncovered pitches? Could Sachin Tendulkar have coped with the pre-war South African googly quartet? How would Viv Richards and Andy Roberts have done in Twenty20 cricket?

However, on the other hand, we know the answers because we WANT to know and we have all watched cricket for so many years. Cricket fans spend endless hours contemplating the counterfactuals of cricket history and we can guess what would happen were any player to be transported into another era. Everyone has their favourites – be they for statistical, aesthetic or other reasons – and they hold those players closer to their hearts than any others.

The narrative of cricket has been forged by its greatest players. From Grace to Trumper, Barnes to Hobbs, Bradman to Compton, Miller to Sobers, Lillee to Richards, Marshall to Akram, Tendulkar to Warne, Kallis to Kohli. All of them – and many more – were the reasons people from all over the world fell in love with cricket and everything it entails.

Acknowledgements

There have been countless publications featuring opinions over nearly two centuries of cricket. My bookshelves are full and many books have helped. There have also been endless conversations with my colleagues, most of whom have had first-hand experience of playing both with and against many of the names featured in these pages.

Particular thanks – in chronological order – are due to a number of people. My parents – for taking me to Lord's at the age of 9, which started my fascination with the game. Mr Chalk appointed me 'scorer' for our school's first three competitive cricket matches at the age of 11, which ensured a neat scorebook, if slight frustration. It was like fielding at short leg – once you demonstrate a certain degree of aptitude, you will never field anywhere else! Fortunately, Mr Charlwood had more faith in my military medium-paced offerings further up the school. All the while, Neil Amswych and Rob Davis ensured plenty of practice on the 'Owzthat' playing field.

Rob Eastaway answered this 12-year-old's letter, which started a long friendship and connection with the ICC World Rankings. Many hours were spent discussing the merits of various players with the team of Ted Dexter, Colin Mayes, Peter Barker and Roger White, not to mention Gordon Vince and his technical expertise.

Melvyn Corin's feats of prodigious run-scoring encouraged me to collect as many of our club's records as possible before 'publishing' them when still in my teens.

Bill James, Rob Neyer, Alan Schwarz and Joe Posnanski all inspired an interest in statistics far beyond what appears in the traditional scorebook, and all have the talent to convey their statistical ideas in understandable prose.

Thanks to Barney Francis for taking a chance on an Accountant-turned-Marketeer-turned-Financial Services Project Manager back in 2006, and to everyone in the SKY Cricket department since then. Mark Lynch probably deserves special praise for having spent the most time on tour in my company than anyone else!

Luke Sutton and everyone at White Owl Books have been a great help and instrumental in bringing these ideas to print. I owe a great deal of thanks to all of them for their advice and encouragement along the way.

Lastly, thanks to William and Oliver, for ensuring life is never dull. And to Joanna, for everything she does and for putting up with us all.

Index of Players Featured